About the Author

Ted Oliver wanted adventure. He wanted it so badly that he sold up a thriving UK business and started over in the USA. As a federal bounty hunter.

Over the next twenty-plus years, he brought in close to 48,000 'skips.' Some came quietly. Some wound up in body-bags. Oliver himself was shot, stabbed, beaten, kidnapped, and thrown into jails along the way.

Oliver's determination to become one of the best undercover federal recovery agents in the USA led him into America's dirtiest, darkest corners to pursue renegades who would rather die than surrender.

A 7th-degree black belt martial artist, Oliver is also an expert in firearms, unarmed combat, and wilderness survival. He is a trained sniper, mercenary, and an FBI contractor.

Website: tedoliverbountyhunter.com
Facebook: Ted Oliver Bounty Hunter

Dead or Alive
Book One
The Beginning

Ted Oliver AKA Dan Durass

Dead or Alive
Book One
The Beginning

Olympia Publishers
London

www.olympiapublishers.com
OLYMPIA PAPERBACK EDITION

A CIP catalogue record for this title is available from the British Library.

ISBN: 978-1-78830-361-3

Although the author and publisher have made every effort to ensure that the information in this book was correct at press time, the author and publisher do not assume and hereby disclaim any liability to any party for any loss, damage, or disruption caused by errors or omissions, whether such errors or omissions result from negligence, accident, or any other cause. The opinions expressed in this work are those of the author and not the publisher

First Published in 2021

Olympia Publishers
Tallis House
2 Tallis Street
London
EC4Y 0AB

Printed in Great Britain

Dedications

People in the States told me I would not live very long with the dangerous career I chose to follow. But here I am today, still alive to tell the real story.

I dedicate this book to my wife Irena, whom I owe so much, who has been at my side for over eighteen years, providing me with constant motivation, adding complete stability to my life, always believing in me, and convincing me that my story was worth telling, with the endless help and encouragement you gave me over the years, even when I had constant flashbacks and relived terrible nightmares. I know it was terrifying for you, having no conception of what was going on with my sanity, but you held me and put up with it when you could have so easily walked away. I could not have survived on my own with what was going on in my mind.
Without you, I dread to think of what I might have become.

I also dedicate this book to my two sons, Cameron and Mindaugas. You have both helped me realise how important it is to belong to a family that I so much longed for. And of course, without you both, I would have finished this book ten years earlier. I truly love you both with all my heart, and I could not have written these books without your support.

In loving memory of my mother, Phyllis, and my father Ernest, I lost both at a very young age.

Acknowledgements

No author has ever written a good book alone. Somewhere along the line, he had some assistance. This book is no exception. I want to thank Alan Wilkinson, who tirelessly spent many months unravelling all my handwritten logs of cases I was working on in the States and slowly putting them together to make some sense for the books finally.

I would also like to thank Clive Corner and Paul Brackley for all the help and guidance they gave me when I first started writing. They helped me get some idea of how to put the books together. Thanks to my secretary, Jo Baxter, who, at short notice, tirelessly spent weeks helping to type up the chapters.

Thanks also to Hugh Byrne for the photographs on both book covers.

Likewise, thanks to Sandy Taylor of Taylor Investigations in Tacoma, Washington. She gave me my first job as an armed private investigator in the States. I relied on her for quick licence plate and information checks when on surveillance or tracking skips. Thanks also to my first bondsman Bernie who took me on to resolve my first-midnight run. This enabled me to find my way forward and helped me become successful in the profession I chose to follow.

Gratitude to the many attorneys — Harvey G. McCraw J.

Razan R. and Steiner B. who all helped get me out of many sticky situations unscathed and without serving too much jail time.

Thanks to the many doctors and nurses that treated me in life or death situations. They helped me pull through.

Special thanks to Dr. Starzl.

I would also like to thank Papa Joe, Ramon, Zoot, Randy, Crusher, Hondo, and all the instructors, who taught me skills to allow me to get through all the challenges I had to complete for my passes in sniping, combat training, and other courses I studied, even though at times I wanted to give up, thinking your teaching was wrong. I now know you were right, and your punishments, skills, and challenging training helped me survive in hazardous situations.

Thanks to my Sensei (teacher) Hirokazu Kanazawa Soke.

Special thanks to all the good friends and acquaintances I lost along the way and to all my team members killed in shoot-outs in this dangerous occupation, standing by me in good, and bad times, notably in life and death situations. Again, I thank you all from the bottom of my heart. You will never be forgotten and will remain in my heart forever.

This book is also dedicated to all the FBI[1] agents I worked closely with and those that covered my ass on many occasions.

---

[1] See glossary

Without your help, I would not be here today.

My admiration to all the FBI undercover and street agents worldwide, who make the FBI what it is today, the best investigative agency in the world.

Appreciation to the FBI. I took all your comments on board when writing these books.

Thanks also to America's professional gang investigators and the intelligence they shared with me. Also, to the sheriff's office, federal agents, DEA[2] agents, and law enforcement, that helped me with information on the cases I was working on. Without your help, it would have been a lot more challenging to resolve my issues, I cannot name you for security reasons, but you will know who you all are when you read these books.

To all my friends out there who are still bounty hunters and to all the agents I do not personally know who are continually involved in this dangerous job: Keep up the excellent work, be careful, don't take unnecessary risks, and defiantly shoot first! Ask and answer questions later. Be safe and remember it's your life that's always on the line.

---

[2] See glossary

Contents

Dead or Alive.
The Beginning
Book One.

Authors' Note

What it took to become a successful
Federal Bail Recovery Agent in the USA.

This first book will give the reader an insight into my background history and the laws I needed to know while working undercover in the States. I had to complete and pass the extensive training programs, the vital information I needed to know, the equipment I used, and how the bail system works.

This book includes some private investigation, bounty hunting, federal bail enforcement cases, and some unlawful incidents in the UK and working undercover in the United States of America.

Plus, some of my very own personal rants.

There is nothing a man cannot do,
when he accepts the fact that there is no God.

There is no hunting like the hunting of man, and those who have hunted armed men long enough and liked it, never care for anything else thereafter.
Ernest Hemingway

Accept me for who I am now, not who I was then.
Ted Oliver

I would like to recommend the reader
of this first book to read book two.

'Dead or Alive'
"How a British bounty hunter took America by storm."
The book will consist of some extremely dangerous
undercover Federal recovery cases that the FBI would rather
I did not disclose, bringing back defendants' dead or alive'.
(See the list of chapters in book two at the back of this book)

***

Three things an agent from the FBI taught me:

NEVER BELIEVE ANYTHING YOU SEE.
TRUST NOBODY.
SHOOT FIRST AND ASK QUESTIONS LATER.

***

Every man's life ends the same way. It is only the details;
of how he lived and how he died that distinguish one man
from another.

Ernest Hemingway

'My Inches in Life'

When you start to get old in life,
things get taken from you; that's part of life.
You only learn that when you start losing things.
You find out that life's this game of inches.
The margin for error is so small.
You know, one-half step too late or too early.
One half a second too slow or too fast, and your life ends.
The inches we need to survive are everywhere, all around us.
They're in every break of this dangerous game.
Every day, every hour, every minute, and every second.
I have always fought so hard for that inch.
I tear myself and everyone around me for pieces of that inch.
I claw with my fingers for that inch!
Because I know, when I add up all those inches,
it's going to make the difference in winning or losing!
Between living and dying!
In any fight, it's the guy that's willing to die,
who's going to win that inch.
And I know if I am going to continue to live this life I lead,
it means I am still willing to fight and die for that inch.
Because that's what living is.
Fighting for the inches in front of your face!

*Adapted from part of Al Pacino's Inch By Inch speech
from Any Given Sunday*

The Two Most Frightening Words A Criminal On The Run Will Ever Hear.

"BOUNTY HUNTER"

Cops are not a criminal's worst nightmare—they need a warrant and probable cause. They also have limited jurisdiction.

Not so for Bail Enforcement Recovery Agents, today's tough bounty hunters, who can cross state lines. They have no limited jurisdiction, they can carry many unusual weapons and equipment, and may use reasonable force in the apprehension of fugitives in interstate flight. They may also break into a property to carry out an arrest without a warrant.

Many people think of bounty hunting as something that was practised in the Wild West and was banished long ago from civilized society. But, it's a fact that bounty hunting goes on today in the US and is perfectly legal. It is an essential part of the American system of justice today.

They operate under the authority of the 1872 Supreme Court Ruling[3].

---

[3] See appendix

PREFACE
Enter the Bounty Hunter

Say the word bounty hunter! And it brings to mind of days long gone by, a cowboy in the old Wild West riding a horse into town, in a long coat, a Winchester lever-action repeating rifle and six-shooter revolver, hunting an outlaw down that is on a wanted poster, for the reward.

In the old Wild West, outlaws like Jesse James and Butch Cassidy roamed the lands, killing people and robbing banks. The local sheriffs did not have the workforce or resources to track them alone or with their deputies. So they would put up 'Wanted' posters, offering huge rewards for their capture or death. Jesse James was worth $5000—big money in those days. Bounty hunters came along, took the reward posters, and tracked the bad guys down relentlessly for that reward money. They did whatever it took to bring in the outlaws, 'dead or alive if necessary.'

Today, the stereotype of the scruffy, unshaven, rogue bounty hunter remains, thanks to television shows and movies.

The modern-day bounty hunter hates this title.

Due to its historical associations, the term 'bounty hunter' is no longer often used or liked by many in the profession. We are much more fugitive recovery agents or bail bond recovery agents. Most modern recovery agents nowadays are fully trained licensed professionals.

The old Wild West free-for-all has now been transformed into a real profitable business, and it is an integral part of the American justice system.

Bounty, from Latin' *bonitos'*, meaning 'goodness.' It is a payment or a reward. Bounty hunting originated in England hundreds of years ago in the thirteenth century. *Bail* was a person, not an amount of money. An individual was the designated custodian of the accused, and if the accused did not return to face his penalty, the designated custodian could be hanged in his place.

During colonial times, America relied on the British 1679 bail system; the British Parliament passed the Habeas Corpus Act[4], which guaranteed that an accused person could be released from prison for a monetary bail amount. And the Habeas Corpus Act was later written into the United States Constitution.

Since the American Civil War, the bounty system has been in use and was an incentive to enlist recruits. Most states paid bounties on timber rattlesnakes and bounties for killing Native Americans: twenty dollars for Indians, eighty dollars for chiefs. And all bounties had a dead-or-alive clause. Bounty hunters supplied most of the prisoners detained in Guantanamo Bay today.

And it's a fact today that bounty hunters catch 95% more criminals than the police. That's because the bounty hunters only track wanted skips[5].

Bounty hunting still goes on today in all parts of America. Most Americans are not even aware of its existence, unless of course, you have a warrant yourself, and you know the bounty hunter is coming for you.

Only a small fraction of people that call themselves bounty hunters have been trained to do the job.

---

[4] See appendix
[5] See Glossary

This Book is Not a Training Manual

Remember, this book is not intended to be any sort of training manual. I don't believe that any training manual, so-called qualified instructor, or bounty hunter training school can train you to do this dangerous profession. A flashy certificate or a pass in those training schools is not worth the paper it's printed on. Some schools will charge you big bucks—that's why they train thousands of novices each year, the trainers know how to get rich from that worthless pass certificate they give you, they also know it will not guarantee to get you a job working in this field, only on-hand experience will.

You will need to learn some exceptional skills: tracking, shooting, self-defense, etc. And I believe the only way to train for this profession is to go out with a bounty hunter who has been working in this field for a long time, learn those skills from a professional, and then try it out your own way. That's the way I did it and how I became so successful.

What this book intends to do, is to inform people about what it was like as a British federal bail enforcer working on his own in the States, tracking down dangerous criminals, getting stabbed, shot at, beaten up, nearly burnt alive, and being kidnapped by gang members that almost cost me my life.

Not forgetting the time I was pinned down with automatic machine-gun fire after tracking a federal skip that had his gangster buddies with him. They blew my truck to pieces with fully automatic machine gun fire; I was hiding behind the front wheel and engine block, hoping not to get hit by a stray bullet. You just cannot imagine the physical and mental state you end up in doing this dangerous job. My nightmares continue every single night to this day, and luckily I survived to tell the story. Well, almost. I want to inform people what sort of background I came from and all the incidents that led up to me giving up my successful business and womanising in the UK to travel to America and become one of the best undercover federal bail agents in the USA.

Judge, Jury, and Executioner

These are a few facts and laws about bounty hunters.

This book is about my real-life experience working in the USA as a 'bounty hunter,' or more formally known as a bail enforcement agent. I worked on federal arrest warrants to pursue America's most wanted fugitives; drug dealers, gangsters, murderers, rapists—in fact, every criminal case you can think of which somebody had been bailed and then fleed justice. My job was to track them down and bring them back, 'Dead or Alive' if necessary.

It makes no difference to me as I still get paid either way. Yet the FBI and DEA would rather I bring some of them back dead, as this saves court and legal costs. It's a very long story to tell, but hopefully, I will fully explain and unravel how it became possible throughout these books. I don't intend to glorify bounty hunting; instead, this is a brutally truthful account of the highs and lows, the stress, the loneliness, the rewards, and inevitable costs, of fighting violent crime, by a lone individual at the very fringes of society.

When I worked in the states, I kept a detailed handwritten log of each case I was working on, in case I was killed by a wanted skip or a fed, as later I found out how corrupt some of their agents were, so that my logs would give a detailed account of cases and names of federal agents I worked with.

I was born in England and lived in the USA, and I became the only 'limey' as the Yanks liked to call me, working legally with a licence in this field.

My books are about the real-life cases I worked on, taken from these logs, original warrants, and case histories.

Newspaper reports, TV reports, and photographs may be added later in books or on my Facebook and website page as proof that this is not fake or fiction.

Rambo

I hadn't been operating stateside for very long before I started to get a reputation.

Guys I worked alongside were making comments about my style. Then there was a newspaper story about this trigger-happy 'limey' coming over and shooting the place up like he was in a Clint Eastwood movie. The way I saw it, I was just taking my job seriously. I wasn't sure that the other bail enforcers were as serious as I was.

If the authorities wanted these bad motherfuckers off the streets, someone would have to play hardball. It seemed to me I was showing these native sons-of-bitches how a bounty hunter ought to conduct himself, and they weren't impressed.

Like the old fart Burton, who states he was America's number one bounty hunter, said in a press cutting about me.

So I became Dirty Harry or Rambo!

At least in their eyes, I did.

Did it bother me? Not one bit.

I'd already earned that same name back home on the safe, gun-free streets of little old England.

I remember reading as press cutting in the states that the American government offered a million-dollar bounty reward for the capture of the Panamanian dictator, Manual Noriega. They called it 'Operation Nifty Package,' they put ten thousand US troops, the Delta Force, Green Berets, Navy Seal commando's, the FBI, and DEA all hunting for him.

I remember seeing Burton doing a TV interview, saying that he was going to Panama after him to bring him in for the one-million-dollar reward!

Not sure how the hell he would bring him back to the states single-handed when bounty hunters have no authority outside the United States.

None of the US authorities could locate Noriega. Later he was found; he had been living at his secretary's apartment in Panama City. They all missed him.

In the end, Noriega surrendered in Nunciature, wearing a shabby uniform with four stars on each shoulder, holding a Bible and a toothbrush in his hands.

No bounty hunter got the one-million-dollar reward money.

INTRODUCTION
How and Why I Started Bounty Hunting

This first book gives the reader an insight into the extensive training I had to complete to stay one step ahead and stay alive, the laws I needed to know, and how the bail system operates in the United States. And how I was able to operate virtually unchecked, unseen, or unheard of in the background. When I brought a case to a conclusion after an arrest or a kill, I would collect my reward or bounty, then disappear back into the shadows, out of public sight with the police, DEA, FBI, etc., taking all the credit.

For many years I kept a sworn secret what I really did in the States. When I stated publicly, I would write these books; I received warnings and threats from the USA's authorities.

So for obvious reasons, I have changed the names of the offenders and law-enforcement officers. I have also altered dates and locations to protect the deceased and families concerned, but all the incidents you will read in these books are real and happened to me in my thirty years' work as a federal bail enforcer.

Until you have been to the States, seen the violent gang murders, drive-by shootings, and high crime rate involving guns and drugs, and worked in this dangerous field, you cannot imagine how dangerous and volatile tracking down bail jumpers is. What seems to be a clear-cut case can quickly escalate to a full-blown shoot-out and become extremely dangerous, and any situation can quickly turn out to be life-threatening.

There are plenty of areas in the States that the police avoid patrolling. The trouble was, I was working mostly in these areas, and I knew if I got into trouble and called for police back-up, they may not come, and I was on my own.

Remember, when I was tracking people down in the States, there were no iPhones, no Internet, no Google maps. All I had was a good sense of direction and the ability to make a quick decision. I could read maps well. A two-inch-thick map book of each city I worked in, and a compass, sat on a unique holder on the car passenger seat. As I drove to find a location, I was continually stopping or flicking through pages and looking at the map book.

In Defence of Bounty Hunting

Bounty hunters and bail bond agents have a bad rap. The American Bar Association calls their line of work 'tawdry,' and Supreme Court Justice Harry Blackmun declared it 'odorous.' But bounty hunters have an unlikely ally: Alex Tabarrok, an economist at George Mason University, who argues in *The Wilson Quarterly* that bounty hunters are 'unsung' heroes of an overbooked justice system.

Bail and bounty hunters have a long history. In medieval England, suspected criminals often had to stew in jail for months until a travelling judge arrived to conduct a trial. In the meantime, the court would release the defendant to a 'surety[6], 'often a friend or brother, who would guarantee that the accused would show up in court. "If the accused failed to show," Tabarrok explains, "the surety would take his place and be judged as if he was the offender that committed the crime." Sureties were, unsurprisingly, given broad powers to chase down their charges; today's bounty hunters have inherited them. They can legally break into their targets' houses, search their property without probable cause, and pursue them across state lines.

Even with those powers, however, the risk of being a surety was too significant—and later on, 'personal surety' was replaced by 'commercial surety,' the system used today in most American states. Under this system, the defendant is released from custody

---

to await his trial in exchange for a sum of money, returned to him when he shows up on the appointed court date. If he doesn't have the money himself, he can hire a bail bond agent to post bail in exchange for an up-front fee, usually around 10%. If a bondsman[7] puts up $6,000 bail and you show up, he keeps your $600. However, if you skip town, he could be out $6,000, so he'll send a bounty hunter after you and will have to pay him the $600 for recovery. Usually, the bondsman has three to six months to find you before the state annexes[8] the bond. All this adds up to big business: The figures show that one out of four defendants doesn't show up for court.

Bounty hunters have a rough-and-tumble image—think of Clint Eastwood in *A Fistful of Dollars*, or, more recently, of A&E's television shows *Dog the Bounty Hunter*. Yet bail bond companies, Tabarrok writes, "are often small family-run businesses—the wife writes the bonds and the husband, the 'bounty hunter,' searches for clients who fail to show up in court." Successful bounty hunters have a combination of 'persistence and politeness.' After all, their targets are their customers, and they track their charges down by working with friends and family. People who won't talk to police will often speak to the bounty hunters, and bounty hunters who are easy to work with will usually get repeat business from defendants. As one defendant-cum-customer puts it, "My family and I have been coming to Franks Bail Bonds for three generations."

The system works, but there are lots of good reasons to dislike the way it works. It can be regressive, penalizing more poverty-stricken defendants; for another, it seems illogical. The goal of the bail bondsman is, after all, to make easy money by

---

[7] See glossary
[8] See glossary

posting bail for poor-but-trustworthy defendants. Why can't the state cut out the middleman, figure out who's trustworthy on its own, and then let those trustworthy defendants go on their own recognizance[9]?

These are sensible objections, and over the last fifty years, most states have experimented with solutions. In many places, a state agency now reviews each defendant, assigning them a score that predicts how likely they are to skip bail; those defendants who have a stable home and work lives are released, while the rest flows into the commercial bail system. Four states (Illinois, Kentucky, Oregon, and Wisconsin) have abolished commercial bail altogether; in those states, the only people with the power to chase fugitives are the already very busy police departments. The government essentially acts as a bail bond[10] firm: it figures out whom to trust and then promises to track down the defendants it's wrong about.

These schemes work—but, Tabarrok writes, they don't work as well as good old-fashioned bounty hunting. Defendants skip bail as much as twenty-eight percent less when bail bond agents and bounty hunters are in place, essentially because bounty hunters are solely focused on finding them. The bottom line is that bail bond firms are more motivated than the state to figure out who's trustworthy and to hunt down those who aren't.

If commercial bail works, then why is it so often opposed? One suspects that the only answer is 'tawdry.' It's hard to reconcile the ideals of justice with the business of money-making, and painful to watch defendants, who are innocent until proven guilty, who end up signing incomprehensible contracts with potentially predatory bail bond firms. At the border of justice and

---

[9] See glossary
[10] See glossary

commerce, it's a tricky balancing act.

When you watch a news story that involves an arrest for a crime, you may hear something said like, "Bail was set at $100,000." Meaning the court has set the bail money, a bond between the accused and the court must be in place before release. Anyone providing a guarantee or surety may also have to enter into a recognizance. These are people prepared to enter into a bond and lose money if the defendant breaks their bail conditions and fails to attend the court date.

Posted by Josh Rothman January 11, 2011, from The Boston Globe.

Now Let Me Tell You How It All Began

Where do you even begin to tell a story like mine?

You first have to look back at my past and the things I did in the UK that led me to take on this dangerous career. When I look back at the things I did to stay alive, it's still hard to believe, but it really happened, and I lived through it.

It was my dream to find a career like this, and it almost cost me my life, but It was my destiny to become a successful federal bail enforcer.

The life I lived in the States was like something out of an adventure movie, but I lived it for real. I have done many things I was not proud of in my life, but looking back, I'm not ashamed of them, and I cannot change what happened.

I remember when I'd been back in the UK for a few weeks' vacation, catching up with old friends and family, I hadn't seen in a while. It was strange to be back in that safe, calm world.

So strange to be so relaxed—although it took me a while to unwind. When you spend every working day building up to a confrontation, never knowing when you're going to be shot or killed, vigilance becomes a habit. But it takes its toll. People were telling me I seemed edgy.

At first, I was surprised. Edgy, to me, meant the way a drug user or a wanted man is edgy. I knew I was none of those; I was in full control I had nothing to be edgy about.

When I flew back to the States, I felt strange all over again. I realised that even though I was pleased to be amongst friends and loved ones back home, something was missing there.

And that something was the adrenaline rush that came when I was at work. I guess you'd call it the thrill of the chase. Someone said to me it must be addictive. I didn't like to hear that. It sounded like a drug, and to me, that was a dirty word.

I decided to launch a campaign. I wanted to work on more federal cases that had come my way from time to time; most bounty hunters won't touch them as they know the immense risks involved, especially if you have a family. I was okay; I had none nearby in the States. I wanted fewer of the nickel-and-dime jobs as I would call primary bounty hunter 10% fees. Not that I was fussy. Work was work, and I always took whatever came along; it all helps to pay the bills.

Starting up again after my vacation, I soon had a full caseload. These were routine jobs bringing in people for 10% fees on misdemeanor offences like; criminal damage, driving without a licence, being intoxicated, making menaces, domestic violence, harassment, that kind of thing. These people were easy to track down. They didn't take off and hide in the woods or out of state. They probably weren't going to come at you armed to the teeth, but you never could be sure of that.

And even though I was only getting 10% of $5000—$500 plus expenses, if I was lucky—the fact that I could sometimes round up eight or ten of them in a single day kept the expenses pot boiling nicely. The thing with bail enforcement tracking work is you have costly overheads—gas, food, lodgings, bribes, at the very least ammo. You have got to keep the money coming in.

One thing that was always on my mind was the fear of death. The only time when it was permissible to use your weapon was if the person you went to arrest was armed and you had reason to believe your life—or someone else's—was in danger before you took the fatal shot to kill them.

Unfortunately, there was no way of knowing for sure what a person's response would be when you came knocking on their door to take them back to jail. Nor did you know when you breached that door whether they would be standing there with a gun to take you out.

I felt that my life in the UK was a test, a preparation to go and do something unique, what most men only dream about, like the things they see in movies and wish they had the guts to do, instead of merely fantasizing about it.

I knew I was different from a young age. Not many people would take all the daring risks and gruesome training I was putting myself through daily in the UK. It was like I was preparing to become something different, something unique, and something sinister that no British guy had ever tried out and lived. It would all soon change my whole life forever.

First, I need to go back quite a few years, so you would understand what made me leave the UK. When I had family, many friends, plenty of money, drove a Rolls Royce, and had a profitable garage business in London.

To sell up everything and leave it all behind, to move to the USA with only my karate training, some private detective training, and of course, my excellent shooting skills.

I suppose it was a bit like the Martin Luther King statement 'I have a Dream.' I have always been a firm believer in following your dreams because one day it will be too late, and you will regret not following your dreams.

I went on so many Del Carnegie courses. They said to make your goals and stick to them; if you don't, they are just dreams, not real goals. So I made a promise to myself, I would follow my dream no matter what I could lose, even my life. And I did!

Bounty Hunters can be Arrested

I wrote this book from my logs of real cases, which I kept hidden for about twenty-plus years while working undercover as a federal bail enforcer, in case I ever got killed while tracking a dangerous skip. It will show and explain modern-day bounty hunting's hard reality and maybe destroy the myth shown in movies today.

It will explain the extraordinary power granted me, to cross state lines without extradition orders, and bring the fugitives back to the jurisdiction they skipped from. I could break and enter into their residence and hold them prisoner until I could deliver them back to the state they skipped from. My job took me to Mexico and Canada, illegally tracking them. I was allowed to carry unusual weapons and devices and travelled state-wide.

You will see it takes a special breed to track down armed skips, bring them back to face trial, and get the bail bond exonerated.

You will come up against dangerous drug gangs, the Mexican cartel, and murderers threatening to kill you. One day! You will need to make that decision to shoot to kill. You will have to put your life on the line! I found at times I even got arrested myself, locked up, and then later bonded out!

I took on all sorts of injuries, including being stabbed, beaten up, pistol-whipped, and an attempt to burn me alive in a burning shack; I have been shot at and continuously threatened with guns. The cases you read may shock you, but remember that they all took place in America between 1978 and the present, where the use of firearms is like going out with change in your pocket. I will also explain the case of a skip I was tracking in another state on a federal warrant, which turned out to be, the most frightening experience I ever came across in all my life. Two gang members kidnapped me, put me into their car at gunpoint, and drove me to a remote area to kill or scare me off hunting their boss. They made me kneel with a gun to my head, and to this day, I still don't know whether they knew their weapon was empty or it failed to go off when they pulled the trigger. They left me there, beaten up and badly injured, but weeks later, I tracked them down and killed them all in a shoot out, including my skip. It then became an everyday occurrence to have guns pointed at me, and the counselling they requested you take after a kill was worthless; I always felt 'I am alive, and they are dead.'

Because of all the situations that took place, people told me that I was like a time bomb, waiting for someone to push the button to explode. Once, in the UK, they tried to section me in a mental institution. Mind you, at times. Even I thought I was losing my mind, and I was turning into a contract killer. So what was wrong with me? Sometimes I would feel so alone, and how sometimes I even thought I was invincible and could survive anything, even death; I would play Russian roulette, and put one bullet in a revolver, then spin the chamber put it to my head, and pull the trigger. Lucky for me, the shell never clicked the firing pin. Why? You may ask. Was I so crazy, and my head was so fucked up? The only answer I could ever give to the question is; Part of it was the thrill of beating death, but part was being ready so that if ever I got cornered by the cartel. A bullet in my head would be better than being slowly tortured by them; it was also to show someone that I was not afraid to die. I used it sometimes to terrify gangsters I had at gunpoint in front of me. I will explain this in 'Dead or Alive' book three.

In the 1978 film 'The Deer hunter,' they showed Russian roulette used on captured American prisoners during the Vietnam War. Still, there is no documented evidence recorded by the Americans, North or South Vietnamese, that this was true. The film also inspired several boys and men worldwide to take their own lives in this same fashion.

It's also not uncommon for bounty hunters to be under arrest themselves when calling for police assistance after a fatal shoot-out. We accept it as part of the procedure, and we, too, have to wait to be bailed out. Surviving those few hours or days in the company of violent hardened criminals taxes the most courageous and extracts a price. I often was put in jail for incidents that happened while I was arresting skips, and I had to wear orange overalls. Remember, I am not above or exempt from the law! The cops and jailors don't care what you do for a living; you are classed equally as a felon. I had to look after myself when the cops placed me in a cell with ten to fifteen other prisoners, but once they knew you could defend yourself, they seemed to stay clear of you and leave you alone.

People told me that I was like a Jekyll and Hyde character. When I was in England, I was calm and peaceful, but sometimes little things would trigger me. In the States, I was a different person; friends noticed that I would get angry and would lose my temper at the slightest thing; I would tell people, "don't ever think that the reason I am peaceful now in the UK is that I have forgotten how to be violent!"

Later, I would have to take a DNA test requested by the FBI before I started working as an undercover contractor, only then to discover that I had a severe problem that I quickly needed to find a way of controlling it.

When I sit down now and think about how my life was, I find it hard to believe it all ever took place. It's like it was a dream or a nightmare! And boy, when I did come back to the UK, it was challenging to find normality, and my re-occurring nightmares would again suddenly start to kick in. I couldn't work out if they were dreams or really happening! Sometimes it felt like I was still in the states, and how I felt when I blew a skip's brains all over the wall, streaming hot blood and flesh that patterned the wall behind him. It was like everything was in slow motion; I stood there in shock at what had just happened. Realising, his bullets had just narrowly passed my head and almost killed me, too! His gun had been fired at me, holding it sideways like the famous gangster way.

This sideways shooting technique goes back to special forces groups deployed to the various banana republics in the late seventies and early eighties. Full automatic machine pistols were prominent at the time, and they were capable of firing in bursts or semi-automatic. Whether used as a back-up or as a small weapon for closer quarters, the recoil from continuous fire caused the barrel to rise off its target. It was problematic for even some competent and experienced combatants. So in cases where multiple targets were close enough together, there was no cause to acquire a target, fire and acquire the next target. All the shooter had to do was turn the machine pistol sideways; this allows the recoil to pull the barrel from one target to the next.

Holding a standard semi-automatic pistol sideways and firing it as gangsters do, would this way make it easier to hit your multiple targets?

I wouldn't advise it, though, as stated by a former Marine Corps marksmanship instructor. I specialize in pistols and have fired these weapons thousands of times. That said, the thought has crossed my mind. The answer didn't come to me until another coach—from the 'hood'—gave me a good reason why gangsters would use this type of shooting technique. In practice, it actually does utilize one essential sighting practice, but it fails overall. It is a good idea in theory, but it fails miserably in the actual execution.

The correct way for accuracy is to line up the gun sights, as trained shooters do. Sight alignment is how you line up the weapon to aim. It would help if you also remembered that the round's trajectory doesn't automatically point at the target—which is why I hate most movies with shooting in them. You have to use control to ensure that both the back and front sights of the weapon are in line and aiming at the target.

I found that the only time I could relax and unwind was when I returned to England, but I couldn't switch off all the traumas and violence in the States. Also, the nightmares continued, and one or two harmful incidents took place in England. I should have seen them coming, but I had no warning what might occur, but I will tell that tale maybe in the next book. Sometimes, I want to go back to the States and carry on where I left off. I miss the action and adrenaline so very much.

1960s to 1980s

Let's start with the sixties-to-eighties span in the UK. Then you could keep all types of weapons at home, as long as you had a steel cabinet to keep them in and a firearms licence or shotgun licence. I had both. I then knew many police officers, and I went shooting at gun ranges with them; I also travelled to many places here and overseas, taking part in police combat shoots.

It was very rare to see British police with guns in those days, and when you did see police officers with guns, it would be because of an armed situation, and it would still only be six-shot revolvers or standard rifles that were issued.

But things were starting to change in the UK dramatically. Hungerford and Dunblane massacres are just two incidents that stand out, making it impossible for individuals to keep firearms. However, you also need to look back at all police fatal errors with guns, but no new law for them.

In the shooting in 1983 of Stephen Waldorf, police tried to cover up their stories of what took place. Waldorf, a film editor, was sitting in the passenger's side of a Mini when armed police walked up and shot him five times; he survived and was later awarded £150,000 in compensation by the Metropolitan Police. It was a case of mistaken identity. Both officers were taken to court for attempted murder and attempted wounding but were cleared of all charges in October 1983?

Then there was the police shooting of another innocent man, Jean Charles da Silva e de Menezes, in 2005, who was fatally shot multiple times in the head on his way to work. On that fateful day, the police were on the lookout for a black Asian, failed bomber called Hussain Osman, and instead shot a white Brazilian man. Another unusual un-tested procedure the police used on that fatal day was 'The Kratos Operation,' which involved not shouting any warning at the suspect before shooting them multiple times in the head and torso. The police also used hollow-point ammunition, which was also very unusual to be in use.

Hollowpoint ammunition was explicitly designed for close quarter shooting in a confined space. These hollow-point bullets would expand when impacting the body, causing massive internal damage instead of like a regular shot that would exit the body. How could the police make such stupid mistakes, kill innocent people, and get away without any police officer charged with murder? You guessed it, only under the 'Terrorism Act.' They say 'The Kratos Operation' is no longer used by the police anymore, although very similar tactics still remain in force today.

The Metropolitan Police were fined £175,000 and ordered to pay £385,000 costs after being convicted of breaching health and safety legislation, In the Menezes case. Still, no police officer has ever faced any charges.

Why is it when one citizen makes a mistake, complete new laws are brought in for everyone in the UK?. But when police make many mistakes, no further rules bought out or any action taken against them, mostly when they kill innocent people? Is it because our lives don't matter to them?

The police were also very sloppy in the seventies and eighties with firearm checks. It stated on the licence how many guns you were allowed to hold and what quantity of ammunition you could keep. When the police called round to do a check on you, they would either give you a call on the phone and give you a date and time they would call round or a review, or knock on the door and say they had come round for a spot check and was it convenient. Then you would make them a coffee and get the girlfriend to have a chat with them while you ran upstairs and took the extra guns and extra ammunition out of the cabinet and hide them all quickly. Then you would give the officer a call, and he would check your weapons and ammo against the certificate and make sure it was correct.

They were never allowed to handle your guns or ammo, only look at them in the cabinet. Nobody checked on shotguns or how many you owned. I had one double-barrelled and four pump-action shotguns and one Franchi SPAS-12—Special Purpose Automatic Shotgun—you could use this shotgun as a pump-action. Still, it was very slow, or you could press the button underneath and turn the gun into a semi-automatic shotgun with rapid firepower.

Now let's go back to things that were happening in my life that made me decide to leave the UK and move to the USA.

Alarms Ringing

My brother owned a car spray shop on a farm in Bedfordshire. He has been there almost soon after he left school. I had to go up and see him one Sunday. It was about 10 a.m. when I got there, the alarms were ringing outside one of the buildings, and it was deafening. He had earplugs in and said that the alarms had been ringing all night and all morning, and the people who owned the unit could not be bothered to come and turn it off. As the farmer wasn't in town, they knew that nobody was going to complain about it. The guy who owned the unit told the other unitholders to go home if it bothered you when they phoned.

"I can shut it off for you, you know," I said to my brother.

"How?" he said, as the alarm was about thirty feet up on the building, and he knew I couldn't climb up there. I asked if he was the only person working today, and he said he was the other units open about 2 p.m.

"Go in and get on with your spray work and leave it with me." A few seconds later, I opened the boot of my Rolls Royce, and inside was most of my guns. I pulled out an M16[11] and a fully loaded magazine; I also took out my Magnum .357 pistol, put it on my waistband, took aim with my M16 rifle at the alarm, and fired off a full clip, blowing the alarm bell and box to smithereens. The bell and the box were still hanging, so I pulled out my .357 Magnum and fired off six rounds. They both came crashing to the

---

[11] See glossary

49

ground smashing in pieces. I put my guns back in the boot. At that point, my brother went out of the garage, shouting, "Fucking hell, Ted, what did you do?"

I said the alarm has now been silenced, so if anyone asks, they were damaged and silent when you arrived this morning!

Miss Luton Contest

I used to go into Luton to a nightclub called Ronnells; I knew the entire door staff. They were all mates, and the manager of the club also knew me as well. I used to jump the queue by pulling up in my Rolls Royce at the front entrance, and throwing the car keys to the doorman, and asking them to park it for me; I used to get a kick from it.

I remember one occasion well. There was a long queue of people waiting outside to go into the club, and there was a large police presence outside the club. In those days, the police had nothing better to do that Friday night, so they came to town and wrote out parking tickets. I pulled up, and a police inspector whom I had had previous run-ins with, as he seemed to hate me because of the car I drove, banged on the window of my Rolls and shouted, "Move it right now!"

I wound down the window and said, "As soon as I drop my passengers off, I will move it."

He then shouted, "Move it this instant, or I will write you a ticket!"

"Fine," I said. "I can afford it, but maybe you can't on your wages, so write me the ticket."

I walked straight into the club and pulled a few friends out from the queue, and I always had two or three young girls in miniskirts sitting next to me at the table. I knew some of the guys in the club were jealous, so I played up to it!

One evening I came into the club after a long day's shooting. I did not want to leave my guns in the car in case they got stolen, so I put them in the handbag of one of the girlfriends I was with at the time. She knocked her handbag over on the bar, and both guns slid down the bar. I casually picked them up and put them back in the handbag, then asked the manager if I could put them in the safe. Most of the older guys hated me and used to say that I was a pimp, only because I had a Rolls Royce and always had young girls hanging on my arms.

I also remember one nightclub. I think it was either 'Sands,' 'The Tropicana Beach,' or 'The Coliseum.' The club changed its name so often. The owner asked me if I wanted to join the judging panel, as a successful Luton businessman, for the 'Miss Luton' competition. I knew the manager and door-staff well, and my Rolls was always parked outside the club's front door. Part of the prize was a trip to a fancy restaurant in my chauffeur-driven Rolls Royce.

I knew most of the girls in the contest, as they were always drinking in the nightclub. When I went into the club to socialize, they would come over and ask me if I would help them win the contest. Of course, I told each one that they would win with my help, but it would cost them, so I took their telephone numbers. Before the final judging took place, it ended up with me taking a different contestant each night down to Stopsley Vale lay-by car park (where the Robinson swimming pool has now been built) for rampant sex in the back of the Rolls, a bit embarrassing on the third night. I was in a compromising position, and we were both naked in the back of the Rolls when there came a hard knock on the steamed-up windows. I wound down the back window, only to find two of the local old bill standing there laughing. Luckily it was two coppers I drank with and knew very well; all they said was, "Sorry Olive, we saw your Rolls parked here a couple of times. We didn't realise what you were using it for."

(The police always called me 'Olive' from the first five

letters printed on my driving licence.) Anyway, to cut a long story short, I got found out as the girl contestants talked with each other, and they reported me; I got spoken to by the club management, and I got thrown off the Final Judging Panel.

Massacre at Hungerford/Michael Ryan

Around August 1987, I was already travelling back and forth, working in the States. I was working outside Reading, fitting up some signs for a sign company in Luton. At the time, I was driving a Mercedes box type van. I had a bulletproof vest and two black holders; inside were a .45 Smith & Wesson semi-auto handgun, a 9mm handgun, an M16 semi-automatic rifle, an AK-47 semi-automatic machine gun[12] , and a pump-action shotgun plus plenty of ammo. I aimed to finish my work and then go shooting at the Bisley camp gun-range. Later that afternoon, I had switched on the radio and heard about the shootings in Hungerford. I think two police officers got shot by a man called Michael Ryan, who had gone on a rampage; he had also hit many other people with two semi-automatic rifles, I think one was an M1 carbine and other handguns. He was dressed in camouflage clothing and had gone on a shooting spree in Hungerford town centre, shooting people at random as he walked through the town's streets. There were no armed police in those days, and the standard police issue firearms were .38 caliber six-shot pistols, which were useless against Ryan's combat weapons.

It was late afternoon, and I had all sorts of thoughts running through my mind. I rang Gerard, my local firearms officer and a good friend at Luton police, asking him if he had heard the news. He said he had, and apparently, they were trying to get a police

---

[12] See glossary

firearms squad to go to the scene, but they were training miles away and had no way getting there as the police helicopter was out of order and was in for repair.

I told him that I had all my weapons, ammo, and equipment with me, and I was going to Hungerford to see if I could help. Gerard, of course, tried to talk me out of it. I hung up the phone and dropped my mate off working with me at the train station, with some excuse about having something urgent to do on my own.

I put on my vest, loaded all my guns, and headed as fast as I could to Hungerford. I think I was about twenty miles away when I suddenly realised that there was a real possibility that Ryan may also kill me too, but I had to stop this madman, and I had the firepower to do it; I was now high on an adrenaline kick.

When I was about three miles from Hungerford, I think it was about 5 p.m.; it came on the news that Ryan had wounded and killed sixteen people and was now in a school and had shot himself in the head. I drove on to Hungerford to make sure the news was correct, but they confirmed that he was dead. I pulled up in a lay-by and breathed a sigh of relief; my hands were trembling at the wheel. Inside my Mercedes, I disarmed myself, taking the clips out of all my weapons, and sat back in the driver's seat; if this had been today with all the CCTV everywhere, I would have defiantly been arrested.

Gerard had been calling me throughout all this time, but I had switched off my Nokia phone. Later that evening, I met up with him for a drink and told him what my intentions were, but I won't go into what was said to me!

The next year parliament brought out the new Firearms (Amendment) Act 1988, which tightened the controls on all firearms possession. They banned all semi-auto rifles, pump-action shotguns, and the use of any shotguns with more than three cartridges. Later came the Dunblane and Cumbria mass shootings. Again, UK lawmakers passed another law, the ban on all handguns' private ownership in Britain, giving the country some of the world's most stringent anti-gun legislation.

There were firearm amnesties all across the UK, resulting in the surrender of thousands of legally held firearms and ammunition rounds. Firearms holders were requested to give up their weapons to the police to be destroyed; they were offered £150 for each gun they gave up. Most of my weapons, including my SPAS-12 automatic shotgun, had cost me over a thousand pounds each to buy.

I never gave the police any of my guns. There was no way I was accepting £150 for each weapon. Did I believe the police would destroy them all? No, I didn't. I remember seeing a press cutting of our shooting club manager giving up all his prize weapons and taking them to the local police station in a wheelbarrow.

My SPAS-12 shotgun and all my other weapons are now safe in my home in the States.

Give that some serious thought?

Skyline Nightclub Fight

Coming back from the States for a break, my new girlfriend and I spent an evening at a friend's nightclub in Luton called Skyline. At the time, I wore a thick ponytail but otherwise was bald. There I bumped into a guy called Martin, who I had once been on speaking terms with but had never liked. Yet he had never done anything before to piss me off. But that night, he did.

He had a stocky build, about six feet six inches tall, a car salesman with his own showroom in Bedfordshire. Most people were scared of him because he had a big loud mouth, especially when he had been drinking; he would pick on people for no reason at all. I was standing at the bar with a drink in my hand, and a couple of times, he bumped into me, pushing his way to the drinks bar and grinning. On the third time he bumped into me, I told him to watch where he was going as it was the third time he had knocked me without even apologising. He just smiled and ignored me and pushed his way to the bar. I followed him and tapped him on the shoulder, and said, "This is the last time I warn you twat, don't bang me again without apologising or else."

He just turned around with a big smirk and said, "Don't fucking warn you pathetic prick, or I will fucking knock you clean out. Oh, and you know what they all say, under every ponytail, there is a fucking arsehole," and he burst out laughing with his mates.

"Okay! outside, you fucking wanker!" I said to him.

"If I go outside, you prick, I will fucking beat the shit out of you and kill you," he said.

"Come on then fucking tough guy, let's go," I said, as I jabbed my finger hard into his chest and walked out in front of him, telling my friends who were the door-men, not to let any of his mates out, as there was going to be a fight, one on one and off the premises. Martin had slammed down his drink and tore off his jacket in a temper.

Outside the nightclub, they had black reflective mirror glass windows. I was standing outside in my light grey suit with my back to the door, I pretended not to see him come out the door and then come running up behind my back, but I could see his reflection in the glass. As he drew his fist back to punch me in the back of my head, I turned and caught his fist with my left hand and punched him under the jaw with my right hand, and used a hard kick into his balls. He hit the floor hard but got up in a raging temper. I told him to stay down and leave it, but he wouldn't listen. He got up and went for me again; I just blocked all his punches hoping he would give up. But now it looked like he really did want to kill me! This time I retaliated with so many punches and kicks.

When he hit the floor again, I followed him down, hitting him with a volley of left and right punches to the face. I heard his jaw crack. His face was covered in blood, and he was screaming, "Please! Please! Stop!" I pulled him up by his collar and looked at him right up to his face, and told him, "Didn't anyone tell you I am a fucking black belt?" I let him drop, then got up to leave, but he got up and grabbed a loose rock in his hand. All I remembered was all hell broking loose, and the next thing I remember was three doormen, one with his arm around my neck trying to pull me off Martin, while shouting, "Ted, stop, you're going to fucking kill him!" I suddenly came to my senses and realised I was holding him by his belt and shirt collar, and I was ramming his head into a brick wall; there was blood everywhere. I dropped him and left him on the ground for his friends to sort him out, then went back into the club to clean up in the manager's office. The staff thought I was very severely hurt as my whole suit was covered in blood, my white socks were red, covered with blood, and my face was thick with blood splattered from him spitting blood at me. As I cleaned myself up in the manager's bathroom, I realised that I had broken my hand and a finger, but because of all the adrenaline flowing through my veins during the fight, I had not noticed or felt any pain.

The next evening, after I had been to the hospital and got my hand and finger in plaster, I had expected the police to come and arrest me, but no one came. I had to meet some friends in the Warden Tavern pub that evening; as I went in the front door, I saw a group of about four car salesmen who were not at the club that night, all turn and stare at me, their eyes following me as I walked to the bar. My mates were in the corner watching. I stopped and walked over to the group and asked what they were staring at and was there a problem; they said, "It was a bit of an unfair fight with Martin the other night."

"How was it unfair?" I replied, "Martin said that you and three mates jumped on him from behind before he could defend himself. You all had him on the ground, beating and kicking the shit out of him." One of them said.

"Get your fucking facts right," I said. "It was just him and me; there were enough people who were looking out of the club window who witnessed it, but if you lot want to start, tell me, and we will go one to one outside right now! Even with a broken hand, I'm still good to fight you all!" But no! They all shook my good hand and said we had heard that it was you on your own but were just checking; they all bought me a drink and told me that it needed someone to bring Martin off his high horse. They said they saw him earlier today and had dark glasses on, as he cannot open his eyes as they were both black, his broken jaw has been wired up, he had two broken ribs, two broken hands, and multiply stitches in his head. "Is that all I did to him? Fuck, I must be slipping," I smiled and said, "Maybe he has learned a valuable lesson. You never know who you are picking on until it's too late. Hopefully, he will start showing people some respect now."

***

I knew I was different after working as an undercover contractor in the states. When I did return to the UK for a break. I regularly did some part-time store detective work for a large store chain in Luton Town centre. It used to piss me off when the shoplifters would come back to the store, not long after they had been arrested and released, and stand outside the store in a gang acting tough shouting, taunting, and swearing at me, making threats that they were going to break my legs, stab me up and so on. I used to stand there with a big smile on my face, not saying a word, just nodding at them; I knew the store security cameras were recording them, and before I left the store that evening; I would go through all the store security records that were saved and find out where they each lived.

Later in the week, I would go to their houses late at night and wait in the dark shadows until they came out to pop to the shop, take the dog for a walk, or go to the pub. I would pull a balaclava and leather gloves on, and then when they came past, grab and beat the living shit out of them; some guessed it was me and went to the police, but I always had an alibi in case the police came to check. That's why I used to stand in the store and always smile; I knew what they had coming later on in the week. After that, they never came back to the store again.

The Car Jumpers

It was my interest in guns that got me into the bounty hunting business. I can't remember a time when I wasn't fascinated with them. It started when we were kids, playing cowboys and Indians. I was always the Lone Ranger, shooting the bad guys as I spurred my horse across the open range, "Hi Ho, Silver away."

But later on, I always wondered what 'Kemosabe' meant, that his sidekick Tonto called him? In Navajo, it means 'soggy shrub.' Perhaps it was an insult? As after all, Tonto means in Spanish' stupid or a fool', but I think it meant 'faithful friend' in the TV series. Other times we'd play Highway Patrol. I was Broderick Crawford, leaning against his 1955 Buick Special with the radio mike to his mouth and a snub-nose .38 at the ready. Ten-four. Guys with guns were everywhere on the TV in those days—and it seemed to me that shooting things was what real men were born to do.

We lived in the south of England, in Bedford. London was barely fifty miles away, but it might have been fifty thousand. Nothing ever happened in Bedford, and if you went out on your push-bike, you were very soon lost among fields and woods. On the face of it, we were just an ordinary poor working-class family, while dad worked as a labourer on the building sites, which was transforming the countryside around us into a vast suburban sprawl. After leaving the Army, he had no proper trade; he took a job as a hod carrier or hoddie, a labourer who had to carry bricks to a bricklayer.

There were five of us kids, plus a stepbrother, but he was a lot older. In school, we were always in deep trouble, mostly for fighting. That's how we settled our arguments in those days, with our fists—or some new wrestling move we'd got off the telly, watching guys like Mick McManus or Jackie Pallo.

Even before I left school at fifteen, I was in trouble with the cops. I got into punch-ups in the street and drove cars that didn't belong to me; even before my sixteenth birthday, I was thrown out of secondary school. Why? Well, the male teacher heard someone talking at the back of the class while writing on the blackboard; he turned and blamed me, then threw the wooden blackboard eraser at me; I ducked, and he missed; I then threw it back, hitting him smack bang in the back of his head, knocking him clean out, as he fell to the floor in a cloud of chalk dust.

They said I was heading for trouble, and they weren't far wrong. All I cared about at that age was cars, girls, and guns— and we'll come to the girls later. At thirteen, I got an air rifle, and I was pretty handy with it. My mates and I would take off over the fields shooting pigeons and rabbits. Sometimes I'd get permission from the farmer, sometimes not. I wasn't satisfied for long. I wanted bigger, better weapons. I read about them, saw them on TV, looked at pictures in magazines, talked about them, and even dreamed about them.

I can't have been more than fourteen when I found the bullets. They were just lying there, in a box in this shed. I dare say I shouldn't have been in there, but I had an inquiring mind— and very little fear. I was desperate to fire them, and I soon figured out a way to do it. I found a steel pipe length took a bloody great hammer, a nail punch, and went to work. I shoved a bullet up the pipe, laid it between two bricks under my foot, lined up the hole-punch, and swung. Boom! Far too much fun—and a good job, there was nobody else around.

I got a shotgun licence at fifteen, then a few years later, a firearms licence. Hard to imagine it with the restrictive laws we have in the UK now, but back then, if you could find it and afford it, you could have it. I ended up with pistols, revolvers, even machine guns—all legal and above board. I started doing target practice on police shooting ranges almost nearly every weekend. I went down to Bisley to shoot. Bisley camp is the place where they hold the annual marksmanship contests for the Army.

Bisley was the home of Britain's very own National Rifle Association. The place had quite a history and a reputation. Samuel Colt, the legendary American firearms manufacturer, produced a version of their famed single-action Army revolver, 'the gun that won the West', and named it the Bisley Model.

If you were looking for one word to describe me back in those days, I'd say I was trigger-happy and an ammoholic. One time I was driving down to Wales to see some friends. I stopped and asked a local farmer if I could shoot the rabbits on his land. It was clear from the look of the fields that they were out of control, so he was happy to oblige. Not so happy half an hour later, when he came galloping across the fields in his wellington boots to see what all the racket was. He found me letting loose with an M16 machine gun. I gave him a couple of dozen dead bunnies to take to market and got the hell away from there.

I tried to keep out of mischief. I joined the rifle and pistol club in Luton. When I left school and went to work, it wasn't long before I discovered I wasn't cut out to take orders. I hated people telling me what to do. I always have done. I had a spell in a chemicals factory and soon made foreman, then left to do a five-year apprenticeship as a motor mechanic. I'd always been interested in cars and wanted to learn everything about them.

Later I would have my own business fixing them up. At the same time, I bought and sold various models of cars, always bigger, always faster, and flashier. It didn't take me long to work my way up to a pair of Rolls Royce's, which I hired out for weddings. The kind of guy I was, I always kept a gun in the glove compartments—usually a .45 or a 9mm semi-automatic, sometimes a .357 Magnum revolver. I remember friends opening the glove box and gasping, "Is that real?" I don't know what I was expecting in those days, but whatever it was, whenever it happened, I would be ready. That was always on my mind.

I mustn't forget my motorbikes. I think that was another career ambition to be a motorbike cop. TV again, putting ideas in my head. I got my first bike at fifteen, a BSA Bantam, like the telegram delivery boys rode. I was underage but didn't give a damn. I was on it and away. Flat out.

Along with all this—guns, cars, bikes—I later developed an interest in martial arts and joined a karate club. Partly, I was inspired by what I saw in films and TV shows, but I was also motivated by the recognition that I needed to learn some self-discipline.

The fact is I had a hair-trigger temper and no control over it. That characteristic—a tendency to give in to total, uncaring rage—has been both a curse and a blessing to many young men throughout history. In specific contexts—in the heat of battle, for example—it's pretty handy. They call it courage and dish out medals for it. Down the pub, in an argument over a game of darts, or a woman, it will land you in trouble. So meditation and martial arts gave me what I needed, the self-assurance that comes with being able to defend myself against almost any assailant, and a controlled outlet for my natural aggression. Very handy, too, if you decide to become a bounty hunter.

I have continued to study martial arts for five decades, and I am now a black belt, seventh Dan. Remember, wearing a Black Belt does not mean you are invincible; it means you never gave up, worked past the pain, overcame the disappointments, and faced your fears. Looking back, I can see I was, in some ways, quite a serious young man.

Driven too. I knew that I had a lot to learn about controlling my aggression. It wasn't until the early nineties that I was DNA tested in the States for the 'MAOA gene' defect. They were doing tests on me, trying to discover why I had this unmanageable, uncontrollable aggression, doing bad things, and not remembering them afterward. I will explain all this later in these books.

I'd left home and was now living in Luton. It was a street of terraced houses, and every mother's son had a car. They were lined up at night, half on the pavement and half off it, nose to tail. If you came home late and wanted to park, you'd better be damned sure you were sober. It was always a tight squeeze, and most of the cars had scuff-marks on the corners. Not that it bothered me. By this time, I had a rented garage a few streets away. I kept the Roller in there. I was living with a girlfriend at the time, but I still couldn't keep my eyes from wandering. Or my hands. So I had this little love nest—I mean in the back of the Rolls in the overnight garage with the doors closed.

The girls loved it. They thought it gave them a bit of class.

This particular Friday evening, I was on my way home after a fling with a very sexy blonde girl I'd met in a bar, and I'd driven her back to her place after a stint in the garage in the Rolls, and was on my way home, on foot. It was late, and everything was quiet. I was trying to come up with a good reason for girlfriend numero uno, as to why I'd stayed out until midnight when I'd told her I was popping out for a quick one. Well, I was—except that she thought I meant a pint of lager. And because it was late, and because even sleepy old Luton had its fair share of hoodlums and thugs, I always had a balaclava in the pocket of my jacket, and I was carrying a baseball bat down the leg of my trousers.

It could have been a gun, but! Well, you have to look after yourself—no good relying on the local constabulary to come to help.

So I was deep in thought about my latest girl as I walked along our street. And then, around the corner at the far end of the road, came a gang of rowdies. They were a mixed bunch: mostly guys and some girls, and they were all drunk as skunks. I should've ignored them. I never go looking for trouble—that's one of the first things they teach you in martial arts—but what I saw as they started making their way down my road made me seethe with rage.

First, one lad, then a second, climbed up onto a car and started hopping from one to the next, kicking up an almighty racket and making bloody great dents in the roofs and anywhere else they landed with their fairy footsteps. They obviously thought it was great fun. They were laughing and shouting and drinking beer, and pretty soon, all of them joined in. There must have been a dozen of them, and they were coming my way, dropping shoes, handbags, and the odd empty beer can onto the road.

We'd seen this sort of thing before in our street and called the local police. Saturday night, they said? You must be joking. We've got better things to do. I suppose I should have walked on by. Was it any of my business? My motor was safely locked away. Why should I worry?

You can't do much about adrenaline. When that kicks in, you

have so much less control. I looked at my hands, and they were shaking. There was a little alleyway connecting our street with the one behind us. I slipped around the corner, into the darkness of the shadows, and put my balaclava on. Then, as the first guy came by, I kept hidden in the shadows, holding the bat with both hands over my shoulder. "Oi you, cunts!" I shouted. "Fucking get off that car now. You cunts! You're causing a fucking lot of damage."

He grinned, laughed, and gave me two fingers. "Fack orff, mate." I didn't argue; I just swung the bat. I caught him right across the shins and knocked him to the ground. He was still rolling around in pain, so I battered him on the head. Then his mate arrived, landing with a thud on the bonnet of a lovely new Cortina.

"You fucking bastards!" I shouted and took a swing at him. "What the fuck d'you think you're playing at, eh? These people pay good money for their motors and look at you. Cunts." I caught this one a glancing blow. He fell to the ground but was on his feet immediately, making a dash for it. I took another swing and hit his back, bringing him to his knees before punching him in the face. Two more of them were trying to clamber over a wall into the safety of someone's garden. I got them both across the back of their legs and brought them down. "I see you around here again—" I punctuated my words with swings of the bat swinging above my head "—you're dead. You got that?" The rest of the gang were already running down the road; as I ran after them, I swatted them like flies.

I was still chasing the last couple down the middle of the road, bat swinging above my head when I heard the squeal of rubber on tarmac, and a car skidded to a halt. Thinking it was the cops, a woman's voice rang out. "Ted! Get in—quick!" I recognised the car and the voice. It was one of my girlfriends, Geena. "The police are coming. Fucking loads of 'em! Come on, will you?" She had the passenger door open.

"Ooh, you little darling," I said and jumped in and kissed her. "I was almost 'TARFU'[13] if you hadn't come by."

"I knew it was you, even with that thing on your head," she said, as I threw my balaclava under the seat. "I mean, who else could it be, you bloody madman? Anyway—" she patted me on the thigh with her hand "—fancy coming back to my place?"

"Not tonight," I said. "No can do. I got to get back to my gaff."

"But what about all those people? Won't they—"

"Listen," I said, "they were attacked by some crazy bastard in black, right?" I slipped off my jacket to reveal a white T-shirt.

She slowed down, drove in a bit of a loop around the neighbouring streets, and re-entered my road from the other end. Some of the gang were still there, one or two sitting on the edge of the pavement, others leaning against the cars they'd damaged. One had blood all down his shirt. A couple of the neighbours were out, talking to the police. There were two or three squad cars and three officers taking notes. One of them flagged us down. "Have you seen anybody running up the road?" he asked. "All dressed in black?"

I shook my head. "No," I said. "What was it, officer? Hit and run?" He waved us away. Two minutes later, Geena was dropping me off a few doors from my house. I kissed her goodnight, said I would see her tomorrow, and watched her drive off.

When I got indoors, I found the girlfriend still up, sitting on the sofa in her nightdress with a cup of tea. "You've been a hell

---

[13] See Glossary

of a time," she said.

"Yeah," I said. "Police stopped and held me up. It seems there was a spot of aggro down the road there."

"So what else is new?" she said.

"Yeah, the usual Friday night thing. Boys having fun. Tell you what, I'm dying for…" I was going to say a beer, then I remembered I was supposed to have been down the pub all this time having a beer.

"What?" She grinned at me. "A quick one before bed?" And before I could answer, she was sitting astride me, sliding her hand down my trousers.

We never had any more trouble in the street after that. Many of the neighbours suspected it was me that sorted them out, but nobody ever said anything to the police. Just that now and then, someone would pass me in the street, nod their head, and mutter, "Thank you."

Shoot-Out on the Streets of Luton

Shoot first, ask questions later. It's a well-known saying that almost a cliché, and it summed up my attitude to a T. I'm talking about the early days before I even realised I had a bad temper, way before I realised it was a serious problem. That would take me years to discover. And of course, then I had to deal with it.

There were two things I couldn't resist in my younger days. One was a sexy, good-looking woman; the other was a violent confrontation—the bloodier and more aggressive, the better.

I was still living in the UK, running my own garage business in London. I was doing well, driving the Rolls Royce and making a lot of money, and since I didn't take kindly to paying a tremendous whack of my earnings in tax, I got people to pay me cash whenever I could. It was a Friday night, and I was driving to my bank, where they had a night safe. I had a bag with about six grand in cash in it.

The street was more or less deserted. The last bus had gone, and the pubs were all closed. It was drizzling and freezing cold. I parked the car opposite the Bank, right opposite the old Co-op, which had closed for business some months previously. I took the 9mm pistol from the glove compartment, checked the gun was loaded and put the silencer on, then slipped it into my waistband under my coat. It seems unlikely now, with all the restrictions on gun ownership, but that was my habit back then—prepared for anything. I got out of the car and glanced up and down the road. I noticed a very old BMW about a hundred yards away. It was parked untidily, two wheels on the pavement at a bit of an angle.

The lights were off, and I could see two people in the front, one or maybe two behind. It seemed odd, but it didn't worry me at first. Not until I heard it fire up and come tearing along the road towards me, still with no lights on.

I shoved the cash-bag into my pocket and drew the pistol. I knew there was a bullet in the chamber. Like I said, being prepared. The car's nose suddenly dipped as the driver slammed the brakes on and swung it towards my Roller. It stopped a few yards away, and three guys jumped out. They all wore balaclavas and caps; in their hands, they had baseball bats. Those were the first two. The third had a crow-bar. They were all running at me, weapons raised.

In a situation like that, there's no time to think. I took aim at the nearest one, steadied myself with both hands on the gun, and opened fire. The first shot took one of their caps off; the second hit the crowbar and kicked it out of another's hand. The third smashed the passengers side window into pieces

The effect was immediate. They all stopped, turned, and ran back to the BMW. "Go on, you fucking chickens!" I shouted, with the pistol still aimed at them, itching to shoot them in the back. "Home to Mummy, you bunch of fucking pussies!" Their car reversed and spun around, wheels spinning in a cloud of smoke. I managed to get five more rounds off, one through the radiator grille, and another through the back window, which shattered into a thousand fragments; the others missed and went through the Co-op window. Then they were off, one door swinging open as they lurched to the left and down a side-road, hissing steam from the radiator.

I stood there in a combat stance for several seconds as they sped away. Suddenly it was tranquil again. I heard a window sliding open somewhere down the road. I hurried to the dropbox and deposited my cash. Putting the gun away, I walked back to the Rolls, stopped, took out my flashlight, and looked around on

71

the ground, picked up all the brass casings from the spent bullets, and put them in my pocket then picked up the crowbar. I opened up the boot, took out my Savage pump-action shotgun, and got in the car with the shotgun across my lap; I made my way up the road in the direction they'd taken in the BMW.

I couldn't believe someone hadn't called the cops. A shoot-out in Luton town centre at midnight? But there was no sign of them. No sign of the BMW either. I cruised around for several minutes and then drove home. I carefully re-loaded the 9mm outside the house and put it back where it lived, in the glove compartment. That was me, always attending to details.

In the house, I showered and changed into my smartest clothes. It might have been late, but I had a hot date with a hot woman. That's how I was in those days. I could engage in a shoot-out one minute and be sweet-talking some woman into bed half an hour later. I took it all in my stride.

The next morning as I drove back to my place, I took a detour past the bank. The only sign that anything had taken place was a few bullet holes in the Co-op window and shattered glass all over the road. A few days after that, I was on edge, constantly expecting a visit from the old bill. It never happened. Today, with CCTV on every street corner, it would have been a different story.

I suppose you could say I'd got into the habit of taking the law into my own hands. That's one way of looking at it. I'd say I was standing on my own two feet, not looking around for someone else to fight my battles for me. Like the time I was threatened with a burglary.

Smoking Guns

It was a Friday night. Some lowlife had just stolen the alarm box from the front of my garage workshop in London. When I rang the alarm people, they reminded me it was a Bank Holiday coming up, and they couldn't get out to me until Tuesday. As I saw it, there was only one option: I'd camp out in the workshop over the weekend. I was dating a model at the time, and I persuaded her to come with me. It would be a bit of a lark. I'd taken her out on a few rabbit-shoots, so she wasn't new to guns, although she was a lousy shot and always jumped when she fired. But this was about frightening off intruders, not killing them.

We took some bedding down there and laid it out in my customer waiting room. I stacked the guns in the corner, under the vending machine. There were a couple of pistols, my shotgun, and an AR-15[14]. I always liked the AR-15 more than its precursor, the M16. A lot of people think AR stands for Assault Rifle. In fact, it's an Armalite Rifle, and 15 is the model number. Manufacturers call them modern sporting rifles, but that's just a way of getting around the laws against assault rifles. They keep adapting it to stay one jump ahead.

My girlfriend of then didn't understand at first why I was so nervous. "Why all the guns?" she asked. I explained it to her. "Look, whoever nicked the alarm box wasn't going to flog it down the Saturday market," I said. "It's a holiday weekend, right?

---

[14] See glossary

They're planning to rob the place. And where does that leave me, eh? No alarm, no insurance pay-out."

That first night was quiet. It put her at ease, but it made me all the tenser, and I was convinced the break-in would happen, and the odds on it happening on Saturday were now shortened considerably.

We went down there early evening and settled in. We ate a picnic supper and drank a bottle of champagne, then settled down under the quilt for a bit of rumpy-pumpy.

It was about 2 a.m. when we were both awoken by a loud crash and the revving of an engine. I grabbed my AR-15, checked my pistol, and handed the girlfriend the shotgun. "If they come this way," I said, "don't ask questions. Just give them both barrels in the air."

I made my way towards the workshop, crept inside, and crouched down behind a car ramp. I could hear scuffling noises. In the darkness, it was hard to tell where from. "Okay, you bastards!" I shouted. "Come out with your fucking hands up, or I'll fire. I've got two guns. Pistol or machine. Take your pick, you thieving little cunts."

No response. Whoever was there was keeping very quiet. "If you wanna fucking die," I said, "it's your call. I'm ready for you, and I am going to open fire on you fuckers." As I fired off one shot with the pistol, that did it. I heard a paint canister clatter to the floor as two or three pairs of feet scampered away. Someone tripped over a trolley-jack and gave a yelp of pain. I opened fire with the AR15, ran to the doorway, and gave it another burst. When I let go of the trigger, I heard tyres squealing from the road outside. I ran out of the yard just in time to see a traveller's beaten-up old van speeding up the road without lights, and I fired off two more rounds in the air as the van turned the corner on two wheels, smoke billowing from the exhaust. I aimed the gun at the drivers' window but resisted the urge to send them on their way with a few more rounds. I didn't want blood on my hands, even if it was the blood of a bunch of fucking thieving crooks. Whoever it was, they wouldn't come back in a hurry.

Back in the workshop, I put on the lights and looked around, just in case.

But there were no bodies or blood. That was a relief. I gave my girlfriend a big hug, and then we put a kettle on and relaxed.

A few minutes later, as we sat there, drinking our tea and watching the last fingers of gun smoke drift away through the open doors, a strange feeling overcame me. It was a moment of self-realisation. What had just happened, I'd loved every minute of it, the action. That was what turned me on. I had never felt more alive than over those few moments when I was blasting away into the darkness.

The following week, I started going through the local newspaper ads. I was sure I'd seen one looking for people to do investigative work. Over the next year, I picked up a job here and a job there, and I went on a couple of courses and learned about observation, surveillance, background research. I attended a few more firearms training courses, but it was never going to be enough to satisfy me. The sort of excitement I craved, chasing people with a gun in my hand, wasn't an everyday event in the dreamy old England. But America? Well, I only had the TV shows and movies to go on, but it seemed to me that over there, they were acting out my fantasy. Cops who were armed to the teeth and licensed to go shoot up the bad guys. That was my dream and what I wanted.

I found out that the central library kept Yellow Pages for individual States in America. I felt I was onto something—as if I was a prospector who'd struck a vein of gold. They weren't allowed to lend them out, so I spent hours in the library, and I photocopied all the pages I needed at ten pence a time.

Then I went home and started writing letters to jobs in the States. Hundreds of them, but not one single one replied.

My Early Years

I didn't get much joy from that first attempt to find a way to the Promised Land. Nobody ever did reply to my letters, not a soul. But the idea had taken root. One day, I told myself, I would just take off. Sell everything I owned in the UK and start anew—one day. Meanwhile, I had other things on my mind.

I'm thinking about women, and what my ex-girlfriend was always telling me, that I was a compulsive womanizer. She was right. I can admit it now, but when I look back, you know what? I don't feel bad about it. Not at all. All I was doing was following my instincts, every regular guy's instincts. You see an attractive female, and no matter what else you're doing, no matter who she happens to be with, one part of your mind imagines that you're in bed with her. You have no control over that at all. It's your subconscious. You may tell yourself you're going to ignore her. You may walk on by and pat yourself on the back because you've got your base desires under control, except that you haven't. They're still alive and well and working overtime. The difference between most other guys and me was that I could not ignore those impulses.

A part of me was at it non-stop, even when I was thinking about other things. Like when I was backing my Rolls into a tight space and some gorgeous woman walked past. Boom, I hit the kerb. Boom, my heart was thumping. Or there was the time when I was walking down the street with the wife—don't ask me which one, because when you've had three, the memories get blurred—

so there I am, walking along arm in arm when my eyes light on some vision of loveliness coming out of a cafe or shop. Suddenly I've got an elbow jabbing me right in the ribs, and it's, "Stop it, you hear?" Believe me; your wife knows what's on your mind, even if you don't—every time.

I've always been good at getting into trouble. It seemed in Bedford if there was a fight or something reported to the police, the 'Oliver house' was where they would come first for questioning, as we always seemed to get the blame. All this started as a kid and got worse when I hit adolescence and developed an interest in sex. Or you could call it a raging obsession. I don't know what my brothers and sisters got up to, but for me, there was only one thing on my mind as I hit adolescence, which was the opposite sex. Why else would I hop on my push-bike one summer morning and pedal five miles out to my girlfriend's dad's farm when we should have been in school? I was fourteen and frustrated. The so-called sex education they gave you at secondary modern only gave you the theory. I was a practical kind of kid. I wanted to bring all those diagrams to life.

So Sharon and I were well on our way to finding out what happened when you get naked and horizontal when her old man came back from milking the cows and wanted to know why she wasn't at school. She was a quick-witted girl. She had shoved me under the bed, groaned piteously, and told him she was taking the day off on account of 'women's troubles.' He grunted and went back to the cowshed.

At that age, I'd do anything if there was a girl around. Like the Sunday afternoon when I was walking around Bedford with a couple of girls. My brother was after one of them. I had the hots for the other, a dark-haired beauty called Karen. Every time I spoke to her, she blushed, and I was already savvy enough to know what that meant. We passed the County Hotel in Bedford, which was still under construction at the time. It was one giant building site, with eight storeys of scaffolding, and at one end of the site a mountain of sand. I don't know whose idea it was to climb to the top floor and jump off, but it seemed to me like a chance to impress the girls, and I jumped at the chance— literally.

Someone had told me that was the key to getting into a girl's knickers: were acts of daring recklessness.

What I hadn't accounted for was that, by the time I'd clambered my way up the scaffolding and several ladders and edged my way nervously along a succession of wobbling planks, some nosy bastard had spotted me and called the cops. So there I was, just like James Cagney in the climactic scene of *White Heat*—the bit where he stands at the top of the blazing distillery and shouts, 'Made it, Ma, top of the world!'

Not that there were any flames involved in my case, nor cops with guns surrounding the site. But the police did show up—in a black Wolseley, with the bells clanging, and they did wave their truncheons as they tried to talk me down.

"All right," I shouted. "I'm coming down." But I hadn't climbed up there for nothing. I could see Karen, way down below, gazing up at me, mouth open. I shut my eyes and went for it. As I sailed through the air with my arms at my side, I could hear screaming below; I remember thinking to myself, 'If this doesn't get her knickers off, I don't know what will.'

I never got the chance to feel her underwear, but I certainly felt mine. When I landed, the impact shoved my pants so far up my arse I nearly choked on them. I sank into the sand right up to my chin. My teeth chipped, my tongue was bleeding, my bones and body were crying out in pain, and I was almost wetting myself as two boys in blue worked their way up the sand-pile on all fours, cursing as their shoes filled up with the stuff. After they'd dug me out, I got a good shaking and a few clips around the ear, and a severe talking-to down at the station. For the next week or two, I carried multi-coloured bruises on my upper arms where they'd put the squeeze on me. After they'd put the fear of God in me, they took me home to my old man, who went to work on me with his trusty leather belt. Happy days.

Royal Blood

You're supposed to grow out of that youthful desire for thrills, excitement, and walking on the edge. I don't think I ever did.

I always liked women. When I think about it, I guess it started with my mother, a wonderfully warm and loving person, whereas my old man was well, let's not beat about the bush. He was a beast. He met my mother in the 1940s when he was fighting the Japanese in Burma with the Buffs. I've read enough about the war in the Far East to have every sympathy with a guy who comes home and can't get the brutality he's experienced out of his head. We all know the Japanese behaved atrociously, they were brainwashed half of them, and they inflicted awful cruelties on their enemies and their prisoners. They were evil bastards faced with an enemy like that, and any soldier will become hardened. They'll become as savage as their enemy. Look at how men behaved in Vietnam. They didn't set off to war determined to do evil. War did it to them. So, yes, I have a degree of understanding of how my old man ended up the way he was. I can understand him coming home and being haunted by what happened in the jungle. Even in my line of work, the things I've witnessed, and the things I've had to do, come back to haunt me. I've had flashbacks, and I still have nightmares. I've woken in the night screaming, with my hands around my wife's throat. Part of living with that is controlling your responses to it. Going and sleeping in the spare room, for example, and seeking help from a counsellor—when you've found one who really understands.

Maybe my old man could've controlled his rage, and perhaps he couldn't. I only know what I saw—and felt. Like the back of his hand, the broomstick across your head, his harsh words, his leather belt. It was the buckle end for us boys, every time. As well as the violence he dished out; there was the hardship. When I was little, he was in and out of work. He was never going to be much more than a labourer on the building sites. If we hit bad weather in winter, he could be out of work for weeks at a time, so we were often short of money. We kids could cope with that. There was always food on the table; we were also sent down to the local market when it was closing time with empty shopping bags; we had to collect all the old fruit and vegetables. These vegetables were lying on the road but cooked up okay and kept us fed, but it must have been tough on Mum because she came from a very good background. How good? Try royalty. Well, that's what she used to tell us. About the servants they had, the elephants inside the palace, the tigers they kept as pets under the table. And we, being kids, just said yeah, yeah, yeah—there she goes again.

It wasn't until after she died that we found out it was true, that she actually had royal blood in her veins. The Burmese king and queen were overthrown way back in the 1880s when the British incorporated the country into its Empire. They went into some kind of exile, and she was one of their descendants. As to how she got involved with a common soldier, I have no idea, but I would guess he represented a chance to escape a war-ravaged country. You hear loads of stories about German women marrying below themselves in order to get out of occupied Europe in the late 1940s. Even today, you have it—all those lovely young Russian women on the Internet looking for old sugar daddies in the West.

It's happened throughout history, and most likely, it always will.

There they were, this odd couple, trying to make a go of it in drab, post-war Britain. Dad was ruling the roost with a rod of iron. He looked like a soldier and acted like one—a sort of drill sergeant, I suppose. He stood five feet eight, stocky and well-muscled. Shoulders back, chest out like a bloody cockerel—Clean-shaven, with cropped blond hair. Always smartly turned out. He pressed his brown demob suit and put that on—or a blazer with his regimental badge and medals if he went to the pub. On a good day, he was quite the lad, cracking jokes and laughing, a fun guy to be around, until his temper flared up, without warning—especially if he'd had a few drinks. It was then us kids that caught it—Ron or me first because the eldest was always to blame the way he saw it. We were supposed to be an example.

We took most of it in our stride. Kids are pretty resilient. If they are born and raised in a pig-sty, they're going to feel at home in a pig-sty, and if they're regularly beaten, they learn to shrug it off, mostly. They shouldn't have to, but they do. It's all they know. Then they grow up, and you hear them say, "It never did me any harm." I probably said it myself. But it does, and the damage starts to show itself when you have to work out how to raise your own kids, how to be a husband and a father. Then what have you got to go on? Only what you know.

I made a promise to myself never to hit a woman or my own kids when I had them. Never.

I learned to shout loud and firm, and that has always been enough. The so-called experts say that shouting is a form of abuse and can damage kids' hearing and brains? But punching or slapping a kid around the head will do more physical damage?

So I put up with what he did to me. It was seeing the old man turn on Mum—that's what got to me, and that I could not abide.

There was just one time when I saw him put his violent temper to good use. A guy who lived up our street went berserk, going round the neighbourhood shouting and bawling, with an axe in his hand. Soon as Dad saw it, he just went out, overpowered the guy, and disarmed him; he never said a word. I don't think he even took anything with him, not even a stick. It was over in a flash. As I remember, he did it with his bare hands. The next day, kids were coming up to me at school, telling me what a hero he was. I felt a brief flush of pride, then confusion. Him? A hero? I was glad when all the fuss died down.

If all the things that happened to us took place now, you'd expect someone to intervene—social services and so on. I'd often turn up at school battered and bruised. Once in a while, my teacher would ask me what I'd been up to. I'd laugh it off and make up some story. "I fell down the stairs, sir." "Trod on the garden rake, didn't I?" "I was sleep-walking, banged into a door." That sort of crap. Pretty soon, they stopped asking. I guess they had their suspicions, but they didn't know what to do. Once or twice a neighbour got onto the NSPCC[15], but we all kept shtum when they sent someone around. If there's one thing that rattles a kid more than his old man going for him with a belt, it's the idea of being sent to live in a kid's home. That used to terrify me.

In the end, I put a stop to it. I must have been about fifteen. I was no bigger than he was, but I'd become defiant. We had a bust-up of some sort, and he punched and knocked me down. I got up. He knocked me down a second time, and up I got again. Over and over again, it happened, until he was standing there with both fists raised and a puzzled look on his face. I stared him down, even as I fought back the tears. "Do what you like," I told him. "You can't

---

[15] See glossary

hurt me no more. But I'll tell you this. You touch Mum one more time, and I'll fucking kill you. Don't ask me how, but I'll find a way while you are sleeping."

I don't know whether Mum knew what had happened, she never mentioned anything about it, but at least until I left home, she was safe from him. Later, Dad suffered a stroke and lost all feeling down the right side of his body. He couldn't walk without a walking frame, and his speech was slurred.

I'm not saying all this to get pity. I'm trying to explain about an empathy I had with the woman who mattered most to me. As for the man who should've been my role model, I held him in contempt. And that affected me in other ways. I had a few mates, of course, I did, but when I wanted company, someone to talk to, I more often found it with girls. They seemed kinder, gentler, and more vulnerable. So maybe that's one reason why I got so interested in them—that and the obvious one that I was a horny little bastard. Girls seemed to me to offer warmth, comfort, and tenderness.

And, of course, the possibility of a fuck.

For that delicious thrill, I would do anything; I suppose— even get married if I had to.

Expensive Mistake

I'd been out of school and working for about a year. I was a trainee motor mechanic. In old money, they were paying me £3, 2s and 6d a week. What's that in new money? About the same: bugger all. It wasn't enough, in those days, to pay the rent on a one-bedroomed flat or cover necessary household expenses. So I did other part-time work, repairing cars at home to make ends meet.

The problem was that I had expensive tastes. Having had nothing as a child, I wanted bright, shiny, expensive things. And I soon found a way to get them. Along with my other interests, I had a passion for guitars. There was no way I could afford a new one, so I scrounged some bits of wood from somewhere and, armed with a few basic skills I'd picked up in woodwork, made my own. I practised for hours in my bedroom. I got pretty good, and before long, a group manager knocked on the door and invited me to join a local band as a rhythm guitarist. 'Los Picaflores.' God knows where the name came from, but that's who we were. It's Spanish.

It means 'The Hummingbirds.' We were an eight-piece outfit: guitars, organ, sax, drums, and a couple of black singers upfront—a guy and a girl. Pretty sophisticated, now that I look back. Maybe ahead of our time. Most bands at that time would be bass, drums, lead guitar, and a singer. I was really into the music. Over the next few years, I played or rehearsed just about every night. Mum came to the weekly shows at the Bedford Corn

Exchange and the Civic theatre, and she decided we needed a 'new look.' She ran up a set of shiny, silky matching shirts for us. We did well, and we started doing gigs all over London. I was soon making thirty to forty pounds a week to add to my regular income.

With all that lovely money in my savings, I was able to indulge another passion—for anything with wheels. Suddenly my trusty old BSA Bantam seemed much too quaint and lightweight, a boy's bike. I wanted something more manly. I got rid of it and bought a Francis Barnett. In rapid succession, I acquired an Ariel Leader, a Royal Enfield 250 Continental, BSA Goldstar, Norton Commando, and a Triumph Bonneville, all of them classics in their own right, and all very collectable in years to come—after I'd sold them. I even built one of my own devising: a Norton Featherbed frame, a Triumph engine, we called it a 'Triton' with a full metallic green fibreglass fairing. It didn't half move.

Back in those days, a motorbike was a real token of manliness. Remember Marlon Brando in *The Wild One*? There was no question; it gave you a head start when it came to pulling the girls. The only problem with motorbikes was they weren't exactly designed for what I had on my mind—namely, sex. You could attract the girls with a bike—but where were you going to go when you wanted to get down to the nitty-gritty?

I bought a car. Later, as I've said, I would get into serious motors—Mercedes, BMWs, Rolls Royces—but I was only starting out. I went to the bottom end of the market. I bought a bubble car. There were quite a number of these three-wheelers around at the time; cheap to buy and cheap to run. They were taxed as motorcycles, so that was another saving. Who can forget the Heinkel, which looked more like a small aircraft—and a German one at that—shorn of its wings? I ended up with an Isetta, two wheels at the front, one at the back, and you got in by lifting the entire front section of the body, which was the door and stepping into a bench seat designed for two. Only the Italians could've come up with that, bless 'em.

I hadn't had it long when I dropped in at the Fox pub with my mate, Dennis, and saw a cracking-looking blonde girl.

"Cor, I don' half fancy her," I said.

"No problem," said my mate. "She's a friend of my sister's. You want me to fix you up?"

He got a free drink for his trouble and, the following weekend, I got a date. I decided to leave the 'Triton' at home and go there in the three-wheeler; I walked into the pub wearing my coolest outfit—tightly fitting ice-blue jeans, a pair of brand new suede shoes—brown, not blue—crisply ironed shirt and a black leather jacket. Step aside, lads, here comes Mister Cool. I spotted Dennis at a corner table and there beside him, with her back to me, the blonde-haired girl. Catching Dennis's eye, I winked at him, then walked up behind her. She looked lovely, flicking her hair aside to reveal a delicately, curved, pale neck. Then she turned to greet me. Oh shit. Wrong fucking blonde, this wasn't the girl I'd spotted the previous week. She seemed a bit mousy.

Well, you know the old saying: a bird in the hand is worth two in the bush. I ordered a round of drinks and started chatting. As she warmed up, we began to have a few laughs, and as she laughed, her face started to seem more appealing. When she got up to go to the Ladies, I noticed that she had a super figure in that little short mini skirt.

By closing time, when I offered her a lift home, we were both well on the way to being pissed. We squeezed into that bench seat, and I drove to a spot I knew where we wouldn't be disturbed, a quiet back-road that led down to the woods—a proper old lovers' lane.

Liz took me by surprise. She was an enthusiastic lover who needed little persuasion. The only difficulty we had was getting our clothes off in that cramped space. We managed. We were young—and what do they say? Love will find a way? We somehow managed to release the handbrake during our contortions, so when the earth moved, it moved for both of us— and only after we'd peaked did we realise that it was still moving. The car rolled down a slope and deeper into the woods, where it hit an exposed root and toppled into a ditch.

We soon got it straightened. Those cars didn't weigh much. But by the time we got back in, we were both lathered in mud. If we thought our troubles were over, however, we were sadly misguided. Not many girls in the mid-1960s were on the pill. I don't think it had been invented that long. And while it was every bloke's responsibility to be prepared, the fact is that even condoms weren't so easy to come by. Sure, every barber's shop stocked them, and we'd all grown up awaiting the happy day when the guy in the white coat would knead the Brylcreem[16] into our hair, brush our collar and ask, "Something for the weekend, sir?" But they wouldn't do that for a seventeen-year-old, no matter how cocky you were. As for going into the chemist's and asking, wow, that took balls. The women in there were old enough to be your mum. There was every chance they'd gone to school with her. We knew they had kids, but there was no way we could imagine them having sex. The idea was as repulsive as it was ridiculous.

So, like a lot of young men like me in those days, I came unprepared. And, like many of her contemporaries, Liz was up

---

[16] See Glossary

the duff. In the club. Fuck me; she was pregnant.

We did the right thing. We both told our parents we were in love and got married. Let them do the sums when the baby arrived. It would be too late then. We fixed a date at Bedford Registry Office, tied the knot, and celebrated with friends and family in the local village hall. With the money I was making from my job and the band, I was able to get a mortgage on a two-bedroomed house. By the time our baby arrived, we'd gathered together a few sticks of furniture and were in.

We named our daughter Chantelle. I fell in love with her right away, but it was Liz who managed all the day-to-day care. I was too busy at work. That was how you did things in those days. She was a great housewife and mother, but the truth is, I was an errant father.

I was way too young to settle down and be loyal to one woman. Liz wasn't stupid. She had her suspicions, and they were confirmed when she convinced me that she would visit her mother for the weekend and would not be home until Sunday night. I fell for it, and Liz caught me red-handed. She walked into the room with her parents—who found their son-in-law with his trousers around his ankles, straddling a bare-assed girl over the kitchen table.

So there I was, eighteen years old, a father, and divorced. I'm happy to say my adulterous adventures didn't destroy Liz. She soon found herself a Yank at the airbase in Alconbury and went to live Stateside. They forged my signature on the visa application to take my daughter out of the UK. I discovered a lot later. I didn't even realise she'd gone until the court contacted me to return my support payments because they did not know where she was, and neither did I.

The airbases at that time were quite an attraction for most of the girls where I grew up. American servicemen were snappy dressers, more fun than the local boys, and seemed to have loads of money to spend. They could dance too. My sister married one and went back to the States with him. It didn't last, but she soon married again, a guy up in Washington State—and that turned out to be very handy for me a few years later.

With Liz re-married and out of the way, I happily reverted to single guy status, and to tell you the truth; I'd never really abandoned it. I now set my sights on big cars and fast women, or was it fast cars and big women? Either way, I was only nineteen when I got my first Jaguar, a Mark 2, and was soon testing the effect it had on the girls I met around town. Magnetic, was the answer—and the rear leather seat took a hammering. But those memories aren't what make the old Jag stick in my mind. It was something else altogether.

It must have been at the weekend because I was alone in the workshop. I was giving the Jag a re-spray, and my mind was only half on the job. The previous day I'd been to see my mum in hospital. She'd had an accident at work, the company where she worked had told me, but I was shocked to see that her face and body were covered in bruises. When I pushed her for answers, she admitted that she'd had another row with my old man—this despite the fact that he'd recently had a stroke. Typically, she made light of it, laughing and joking with the several family members gathered around the bed.

When they all left, and when we were alone, she began to cry. She put her arms around me and told me, "Please! Look after Ernie, won't you?" I knew she cared for the old bastard, despite the way he treated her. I never could understand it, but that's some women for you. Loyal to a fault. "Don't be daft," I said, "you'll be out of here in a day or two."

She didn't listen. "Promise me you'll be strong and watch over all the family," she said.

"Don't worry, and stop being silly, Mum; you'll be out of here soon; I will come and see you tomorrow night," I said.

She knew and was trying to tell me she was dying, but I didn't get it. So the call I got next afternoon, as I stood there in my workshop, mask pushed back on my forehead, spray gun in my hand, was a terrible shock; my legs almost buckled from under me. It was someone from the hospital, telling me my mother had died. It turned out that she had leukaemia. The accident—and, I dare say, the beatings—had only precipitated the inevitable.

And the only thing that still sits on my mind to this day is. 'I never told her how much I loved her.'

I carried out her wishes, doing my best I could to watch out for the old man until his death a few years later. There were always a lot of Buddha statues around our house, as Mum was a dedicated Buddhist. When we were clearing the place out after they both died, we realised that the prominent Buddha statue, made of brass, which always sat on the fireplace mantel, had a false bottom underneath that had a sort of screw-off cap. We undid it to find hundreds of neatly folded up notes inside it, each one asking the Buddha to make Ernie (dad) well again and keep the family safe and well. After all the pain and hell he put her through, we thought, she must have really and truly loved him. As for Mum, we still talk. She's like the God I never knew, the person I pray to when I'm in trouble. Whenever I've faced a particularly difficult or dangerous situation, I have always asked her to watch out for me.

And I believe she does—every time.

I now had no real responsibilities to worry about; I indulged myself, shamelessly, in shooting, hunting, cars, women—and I developed a new interest. I was already getting into karate when I noticed that the best-looking girls were hanging out with the black belts. Right, I thought, that's me. That's what I need to do. I worked my way up through the grades to become a first Dan, eventually a third, and so on.

Soon lots of young girls in mini-skirts were waiting and watching me while I was teaching a karate class, some became students, but it wasn't long that before I went home each night after teaching, I was fucking a different girl or student in the back of my car, in the car park at the back of the sports arena

In here, we had set up our dojo, as a karate training ring is called. Later on, I would open my own karate club and acquire the nickname 'Grasshopper' after the guy on the television series 'Kung-Fu.'

I wasn't single for long. One night, I was driving back from Ampthill, when I stopped for two girls in short skirts, who were hitching a lift; in those days, the miniskirt does it every time. They were both student teachers. I took a fancy to one of them and asked her out. Sara had mixed parentage, like me. Her father was Canadian, her mother Indian. She had long black hair and pale brown skin. And as trouble then always seemed to follow me, she called me a 'Townie.' It was a nickname for someone that was not in their college but from the town. One night, she had sneaked me into her dorm at the teachers' training college in Polhill Avenue in Bedford. While we were getting down to the nitty-gritty, I heard a girl screaming from the dorm below. Sara informed me that it was her friend Paula and that her boyfriend was always beating her up, and because he was six feet two, stocky and aggressive, nobody dared intervene or get involved! That was it for me. I jumped out of bed, got dressed on the next scream I heard, ran down the hall stairs, kicked in the door, found this big tough guy punching this girl, and I literally grabbed him by his hair and threw him out into the stairwell and kicked him down every flight of stairs, followed with a punch in his face. I think there were six flights of stairs and then threw him out the door with a karate sidekick to follow.

A few days later, they were back together, saying I was the bad person for beating him up so badly!

Anyway, Sara and I had hit it off very well in bed, and, being young and impulsive—and unable to learn from previous mistakes—I soon asked her to marry me. I got my karate club students to come down to the church in Bourne, Lincolnshire, and punch a karate archway in white karate gi's (suits), as we left the church, married.

I had realised by now that working for someone else wasn't what I was cut out to do. I decided it was time for me to set up my own business. I found premises suitable for conversion to a garage and workshop, went to the bank, and pledged the house against a loan, which enabled me to buy it. I did well. Very well, indeed. Within two years, I had: three garage repair shops, an MOT station, a wedding car hire service, a boasting two Rolls Royce's, a Mercedes, and a long wheelbase Granada. Plus, I was working self-employed in the evenings doing my private investigation work.

The business continued to multiply. I soon had twenty mechanics working for me and money coming out of my ears. It wasn't enough. I really wanted to put into practice all the skills I was learning at the gun ranges. I wanted excitement, danger, thrills. I had all these guns, which I was carrying round in the car, and I wanted to use them whenever I could. But, something was continually eating me away inside; I would get angry at the slightest thing.

One Sunday afternoon, the urge to use my guns got the better of me. I packed some of my arsenal and took off to the yard. I had a .45 pistol, a 9mm pistol, an AR-15 rifle, and a pump-action shotgun. About ten or twelve mechanics were working for me that Sunday, and over in the corner of the garage was a clapped-out old BMW. We'd been stripping it for spare parts, and it was on its way to the scrap yard.

I closed the main doors and told the lads to take a break in the little canteen we had for staff and customers. Then I pulled out my guns, made sure they were all loaded, and lined them up on a work-bench. One by one, I emptied the weapons into the BMW. First, the pistols—bullets were pinging everywhere, glass flying—then the shotgun, then the machine gun. Shit, it felt so good. The noise was deafening and fantastic, there was smoke everywhere, and the car was riddled with bullet holes. As I lay the machine gun back down on the bench, I realised the lads had all come out of the canteen. Some of them looked terrified; they thought I'd gone crazy or something. One or two had run out into the street and were standing there, mouths open. Then one of them, nicknamed Deuce, asked the question. "What the hell you doing, boss?"

I told him the truth that I'd always wanted to shoot up a car the way they did in the old gangster movies—just to see what it felt like; I was fantastic. "Now I know something you don't," I said and gathered up my guns. But boy, did I feel a lot better now! I was on a high I was ecstatic.

That's when one of them pointed out my big mistake. It was an expensive one. Right behind what was left of the bullet-riddled BMW was our entire stock of new car exhausts, ripped to shreds in the stock room. I shrugged it off at the time, but the following morning had to write a large cheque out of my own bank account—first the pleasure, then the pain.

My problem was one that most people would die for. Money. I had too much of it. It made me a bit lazy and self-indulgent. The garage business was almost looking after itself, and with the bits of private investigation work I was now getting, I was awash with cash. I'd always liked a good time, and now there was nothing to stop me from having it. I had time on my hands, and I let it slip by in an endless round of drinking, sex, partying, and holidays abroad with any woman I fancied. I was out every night, going from pub to club in my Roller, and way into the small hours until the last place where I could get a drink and pick up another woman. Some of the pubs used to let us and off duty police drink after hours behind closed doors. While it was happening, it was great. I'm talking years here. But when it started to get out of hand, I was the last person to see that. I didn't notice that I was attracting people who said they were my friends but who were only coming along for the ride—often in my Rolls Royce. These were classic hangers-on, people who were getting their drinks tab paid up at the end of the night, and after I'd gone home with the best-looking woman, they would pick up the leftovers.

I found I was waking up some mornings with a woman whose name I didn't know and whose face I barely recognised. Somewhere along the line, my wife, Sara, moved out after discovering I was regularly fucking her married best friend while she was teaching at school.

After one epic pub crawl, I remember going around all the car parks the next morning looking for my Roller and finally finding it, sitting there in splendid isolation doors open with the keys still in the ignition.

I continued to drink recklessly. One night I made a bet with a friend. We were in the Casa Bianca restaurant in Castle Street when we had the bright idea of seeing which of us would still be standing after taking a shot of everything along the top shelf above the bar. We must have consumed a pint of raw spirits apiece—all in the name of having a good time—no great surprise when I was rushed to the hospital a few weeks later.

The problem? Only that my liver had packed up.

It took me eight weeks to wake up and smell the coffee—literally. That's how long I was in a coma. Then I saw the bright light—again, quite literally. Sometime, during that long spell of unconsciousness, I distinctly heard voices around me and felt myself floating through the darkness towards a bright white light in the far distance. I never reached it, and to this day, I give thanks that I didn't. I don't think it would have been a good outcome.

I remember that when I came out of the coma, lots of girlfriends were standing around my bed. I heard later when the doctor asked who my partner was, they all said they were, and the choice went to Kate, the youngest and the only one that still had my house keys.

So, despite my best attempts to drink myself to death, I was alive, but I can't say I felt great about it. I was weak as a kitten and mentally depressed. When the hospital discharged me, my old girlfriend moved back in to look after me. I remember her putting me to bed that first night and getting in beside me, just to hold me close. I realised then that this woman was a true friend.

I'd had a warning. I'd gone right to the edge and looked over. All the time I was in that coma, my life had been hanging by a thin thread. During my recovery, I had plenty of time to think about things. I resolved to cut out the drinking, get back to the gym and set my stall out to go to the States. I would build a new life, doing the thing that most excited me.

As anybody will tell you halfway through January, it's one thing to make a resolution, another thing altogether to stick to it. But I did. Barely a year after getting out of the hospital, I'd sold all my businesses, my house, my cars, tidied up my affairs, and bought a plane ticket to Seattle, where my tight-assed gambling addict sister lived, that ended up costing me a lot of money, nicknamed 'Pull Tab,' but that's another story.

I would go to Seattle for a holiday and stay with my sister. I asked my ex-girlfriend if she wanted to travel with me; she had a think, told me straight that there was no way she'd reinstate me as her lover, and then agreed to come. She laid it on the line: she was very fond of me and wanted to remain a friend, but she had no illusions about my ability to be faithful. I was, she told me, a hopeless case.

Later, I travelled back and forth to the States many times, setting up my future and planning the new road that lay ahead of me.

I then met and married Rose, an ex-Traveller I met at a night club in Luton. What a fucking nightmare that marriage turned out to be. They nicknamed her 'the human pin cushion!' Now I know why! She was always full of little pricks! After we married, her parents told me that she used to leave her two small young baby boys alone and sneak out of the window at night and go to nightclubs. The parents would regularly discover her coming home in the early hours of the morning; and find that the kids had been locked inside the house, home alone.

Later, while working in the states, I found out she was doing escort work regularly with Callie with her best friend. And I married this piece of shit, thinking I could change her, but that was an impossible thing to do.

I remember one guy from Farley Hill, who was booking her

regularly while I was away working in the States. When he found out that I had traced his name, address, telephone number, and date of birth, his old man said he went white as a sheet after discovering who I was, and I did for a living, and I told him I was coming after him to cut his balls off. He packed his suitcase and went into hiding for over nine months in Blackpool. What a wanker!

Later in these books, I will explain the saying 'Keep your friends close, and your enemies closer.' It's a very wise saying. I'm a professional tracker; I know to this day where all my enemies are, paybacks are a bitch but very enjoyable and 100% guaranteed to follow one day! But that's another later story.

The Beginning in the States

When I was living in the States, I also worked as a freelance armed Private Detective. I was also contracted to work as armed security at the Goodwill Games in Seattle; Intelligence had warned that there was a possibility that terrorists had planned to attack the athletes at the games. Two thousand three hundred athletes attended from fifty-four countries, and former president Ronald Reagan gave a speech. Arnold Schwarzenegger was there, the Moody Blues, Gorky Park, and Kenny Gee played songs. I remember seeing all the kids in pink baseball caps, but there were no serious incidents, and my team had a trouble-free day at the games.

One of the first things I realised when I got to the States was that a British accent would take you a long way. Nearly everybody I spoke to wanted to know where I was from.

And the American women were all telling me I had a cute accent, and 'You're not from around here.' Talk about making a guy feel welcome. I found that American women weren't shy about letting you know they were available, and even if they were engaged, they would still go out on a date with you. They would have you in bed before you even got around to fixing up a second date. I soon got involved with many women, including a blonde girl called Chevy, whom I met at the bowling alley, who thought she was Madonna and kept saying she was a Madonna wannabe. She looked like Madonna, acted, dressed, and danced like Madonna, which was great for me as I was a crazy fan of

Madonna, which helped me play out my fantasy in bed with my very own Madonna!

America suited me fine. The Seattle area has many young people who have travelled there from other parts looking for a new life. It has the energy to it. I felt sure I had a future there. I started calling some of the agencies that advertised for investigative work and learned that I would be better off if I had resident status. If that's what it took, fine. I got my daughter, who still held her American citizenship, to petition for me to get a Green Card so that I could live and work in the States. When I went back to England to put my affairs in order, I asked Chevy to look around Washington for a place I could live.

Things moved extremely fast. I found work with Taylor Investigations, run by a very professional woman called Sandy Taylor over in Tacoma—about thirty miles south of Seattle at the far end of Puget Sound. She was in her forties, married, with a family. Beneath a very jocular exterior, she was a very shrewd operator, and under her nicely cut business suit, she carried a small-caliber handgun in a waist holster. Her father founded the company, Keith Taylor, some twenty years previously, and she was gradually taking it over. It was he who called me in for an interview. Kieth said he was a pilot stationed at Alconbury airbase during the war, and when he spotted my details, he recognized the names of his old haunts on my CV. He still held the Brits in high regard and recommended that Sandy take me on—subject to confirmation that I was all I claimed to be.

With the prospect of a steady income, I was able to look for somewhere a bit better to live. Chevy and I had been hitting it off really well, so we decided to buy a place together. She was a realtor for McPherson Real Estates, and she found the house, which I purchased on a deed of trust terms. The house was in

Auburn, just south of Seattle, a lovely three-bedroom ranch-style house with a drive-in garage. There were a few administrative details to tidy up, like getting my alien and concealed gun permits. Once that was in place, I was ready to begin my new career in investigation and detection.

There was plenty enough work to pay the bills, but it never looked like giving me what I was after. I mean excitement, the thrill of the chase. When I was a kid, and people asked me what I wanted to be when I grew up, I had a different answer every week. It would be an American cop, a cowboy, a Hollywood stuntman, or a Commando. Take your pick. But it was nearly always some job that involved firearms or self-defence. I wanted to be the guy with the gun in his hand, bringing people to justice—and exercising my skills in martial arts. And I wanted to be a lone operator. I never was, and never would be, a team player.

All this was playing on my mind during those first few months in the States when I sleuthed around for private clients on civil matters. When it wasn't some small person in business who suspected his employees were ripping him off, it would be a guy who thought his wife was cheating on him or some woman with an errant husband, or a family trying to trace a missing child. I wasn't complaining. It brought home the bacon.

But excitement? The thrill of the chase? No! There was precious little of that.

I was mostly sitting in my car someplace eating cold pizza, regularly cleaning my guns, drinking tepid coffee from a Thermos, and pissing into the screw-top container I always had with me. I learned that the hard way, having almost burst my bladder while waiting for some guy to break cover from his girlfriend's house. So I wasn't exactly living the American Dream. Not my dream, anyway. I needed a break.

I needed to get lucky.

I was in a bar one evening, sitting on my own, not far from where I was living at the time, in Federal Way, Washington. It must have been about eleven. I was ready to call it a night and head back to my place. It had been a long day in the Seattle suburbs, staring at some divorcee's front door for ten solid hours, hoping she'd get off her fat ass and take a trip somewhere. The video shop, grocery store, the movie theatre, the hairdresser—any damned where so long as it gave me a change of scenery. She never did, and when I saw her putting her lights out, I called it a day and headed for this bar called Jacks to have a beer and a whiskey. I will tell you later in my second book, how this spontaneous trip changed my whole life in a different direction.

All this time, I was still doggedly phoning bail bonding companies all over the state and beyond, trying to get work but always getting that same standard-issue response.

I was constantly battling with myself to stay calm. I wrote hundreds of letters too—there was no Internet in those days and sent them out with a CV attached. I checked my mailbox religiously, every damned day. Not a single reply. Not one. Nada.

Choosing to be a bounty hunter—well, you don't do that if you want a quiet life, do you? And even amongst that motley assortment of characters that do the police's dirty work for them, I seemed to attract more trouble than anybody else.

PI Work. (USA) Paedophile Case

This new work I was engaged in made a lot of demands on me. You might say that anyone with half a brain could acquire the skills relating to awareness, personal safety, arms, and the law. Most people can, in the right circumstances, develop that animal instinct for survival. But if one attribute I found challenging, it was the business of learning to control my feelings and remain emotionally detached. Think about it: you're called on to deal with vicious, sadistic, inhuman people who are capable of doing terrible things to adults or kids and laughing about it. You come across someone like that, and your emotions can run riot—especially mine when you're face to face or having to tolerate their presence on a road trip. Keeping a lid on your feelings had never come naturally to me, and I quickly realised I needed to learn how to do it. The fact is I had to work at that. Whatever our job is, we are, first of all, human beings. I had a degree of self-knowledge when I first started. I knew, for example, that I would never be the world's greatest husband or father. I knew that my dick was inclined to rule my head. But I had a daughter. I never saw much of her once her mother had taken her to live in the states, so I wasn't around to protect her if required, but I knew I had natural parental instincts. I knew what it was like to be beaten as a kid, and if there's one thing I never could abide, it's the mistreatment of children. When I hear of people abusing little ones, it makes my fucking blood boil.

Early on in my time as a private investigator, Sandy offered me the case of a known child molester, who had just been let out on parole. "Give it to someone else," I said. She asked me why, and to my regret, I couldn't find the right answer. I knew what I wanted to say, that I feared I would kill the lousy son-of-a-bitch if I laid my hands on him, but I let it go and took on the job. Maybe I thought I would learn something.

This guy had served time, and now that he'd been released, the prison service wanted to keep an eye on him. It's common enough for this to happen, but as a rule, the police have too much on their hands to pick up a job like that. It can consume a lot of working hours. So it comes to the PI's. This particular subject had been let out of jail on the condition that he went to live in some kind of hostel for a while. I was supposed to watch him, see what he got up to during daylight hours, and report his movements when he was allowed out. I took a dislike to the guy the moment I saw him. He was in his late forties, medium height, skinny, a bony face, a long straggly beard, and small, sunken eyes. The first thing he did when he went to live in this hostel was to get a car. Christ knows how he got it, or how he paid for it, but there he was, cruising around Portland, Oregon, in a beat-up cream-coloured Ford station wagon with fake wood panels on the side.

The first couple of days, he hardly went further than the local 7-11 store. Later he started hanging out at a bar, where he seemed to spend most of the day. Not evenings, though: he was on curfew. Jesus, it was tedious work for me. Only the thought that I was getting paid made it tolerable.

I think it was on the fifth or sixth day that the pattern changed. It was a Monday. I'd spent the entire damned morning parked across the road, bored out of my skull, telling myself there were worse things than getting fifty bucks an hour for sitting there doing nothing. It was pretty much the same thing in the afternoon:

nothing to report until around three when he came out of the house and took off in the station wagon.

I followed him until he pulled up by a schoolyard and sat there, watching the children coming out. I observed him from a distance, through my binoculars, and took a few photos with my long-lens camera. These are things you have with you as standard whenever you do surveillance. With a close-up view of the guy, I could see he was paying particular attention to the young girls; these were elementary school girls, fifth graders, maybe ten, eleven years old. I was bristling with anger already. Then around three forty-five after the last of the kids had gone, he went home.

He carried on like this for the rest of the week, same school, and at the same time. They were hard days. I don't know how I managed it, sitting there and watching when my gut instinct was to get out of the car and collar the guy. I even found myself pointing the finger at him and imagining that I was blowing him away. Why are these people let loose? Did I ask myself? I'd been reading up on child molesters and, to my horror, saw that as many as 90% would re-offend, despite the fact that they're supposed to have had some kind of therapy in prison. This guy was showing every sign of going down that road.

The facts convinced me that he was a danger to any young girl. I knew I had to keep closer to him, but at the same time, I was aware that I couldn't get him arrested on suspicion. I decided I needed to keep him on a tighter rein. I waited until he was back in the hostel, sneaked up to his car, and attached a tracking device to the inside of the rear fender (bumper). It turned out to be a good move.

The very next morning, he set off early. Early for him, that is. It was eight o'clock, a Saturday. I'd changed my car, just in case he might have spotted me, although he didn't look the type to take much notice of what was going on around him. He seemed preoccupied. I followed him as he headed out of town on Interstate 5. I wondered where the hell he was going. He drove for two hours, and I remember checking the fuel gauge. Thankfully, I'd rented one with a full tank of gas. He finally came off at the city of Edmonton. He seemed to know exactly where he was going. There was no uncertainty, no pulling over to check the map. He just made his way straight down the fast-food strip then to a motel. I watched from the car as he checked in and then went to his room. It was one of those cheap places where all the rooms are on the ground floor, and you park your car right outside your room.

He came out a couple of hours later. He'd changed into a pair of old jeans and a long winter coat, which was odd, seeing that it was a pleasant spring day. Not hot, but not winter coat weather. He drove a mile or two back towards town, pulled up beside a park, and got out. I grabbed what I needed and prepared to tail him on foot, moving discreetly from tree to tree.

He got to a spot where they had a few benches. A large group of kids was playing softball. I couldn't see any supervising adults about the place. The kids were young, ten to twelve years old at a guess, and they had a bunch of younger ones watching. One of them was a little blonde girl. She couldn't have been more than seven or eight. The guy had spotted her and couldn't seem to take his eyes off her.

I sat there hidden inside some bushes for maybe an hour, watching, wondering what the hell to do. I knew damned well what I was feeling, but I kept reminding myself of my responsibilities and the law. Then, to my horror, I saw the girl say goodbye to her friends and make her way towards the park exit. I looked around to see whether a brother or big sister was waiting for her, but couldn't see anybody. As she headed to the gate, the guy stood up and followed her. Jesus, I couldn't believe what I was seeing: he was zipping up his fly.

I thought the kid was heading to the road, but I was wrong. She was making her way towards a little cluster of trees, and the guy was still following her. I hurried towards him as he gained on her.

The truth is, I had no plan of action. I was aware that the police could not take any action unless a crime had been committed, but there was no way I could stand there, let it happen and then apprehend the guy. Instinct took over, sheer gut instinct fuelled by revulsion.

I was hurrying now, anxious to get as close as possible but still trying to keep undercover; the girl was walking through the trees now, so I was only getting glimpses of her bare legs between the trunks. Then I got lucky—at least, I thought I had. He called across, "Hey kid, can you help me find my little dog? She just slipped the leash. She's only a pup." He was holding a dog's lead up at her.

I was now almost running from tree to tree, but he hadn't spotted me—or heard me. I was grateful for the breeze that was rustling the foliage.

"Sure," she said, turning to face the guy. She looked worried. She already cared about the lying toerag's lost dog.

"Yeah," he said, "I think she went over there," and now he pointed into the middle of the wood, where the trees were all closely packed and surrounded by low-growing shrubs. "We can call her." And with that, he shouted out, "Cin-deee! Cin-deee!" and walked towards her. He was within a few feet by now.

That was it for me. The nonce had gone far enough; I couldn't hold myself back any longer; I put my shades back into my pocket (sunglasses), I quickly put my rolled-up balaclava on my head, I ran flat out, towards the kid. "It's okay!" I shouted. "I've found his dog. You run home—go on, quickly now!" At first, she hesitated. I scowled at her and waved my arm. So what if I frightened her? I had no choice. "Go on!" I growled. "Git, now! Ya hear me?"

As she turned away, then broke into a run, I quickly pulled the balaclava over my face. I stared right into the guy's eyes. He read my mood and my intentions immediately. He ran out from the trees towards where he'd left his car. He was going as fast as he could, arms pumping, coat flapping, but he was no match for me. It took but a few strides for me to get close enough to grab his hair and drag him back towards the cover of the trees, where I threw him to the ground.

I checked to see what had happened to the little girl. There she was, making her way through the park gate. She was with a friend now and told her what had happened, turning to point in my direction; I waited until the pair of them disappeared, then rammed the guy's head against a tree trunk. He yelled out in pain and started pleading with me. "Lemme alone, I wasn't gonna—."

"Shut the fuck up," I told him and whacked his head into the tree again. And then a cold rage overtook me. I hit him once, twice, three times, full in the face with my fist. His nose was misshapen, and blood was running from his head, "Pick on little kids, would you?" I gasped. "Well, listen up, mister. You're gonna be famous. I've got photographs of you trying to abduct her." I punctuated my words with a kick in the groin. I was struggling with an urge to pull out my gun and do away with the lowlife bastard. Instead, I twisted his hand around; until I heard the bones crack. He let out a short high-pitched scream, then started crying and whimpering like an injured dog.

"You got no right," he said. "I... I'll call the cops."

I gave his hand another twist. "You do that," I said, "and I will hunt you down and put a bullet between your eyes. Like this." I pulled out my gun and cocked it. "Adios," I said as I gently squeezed but stopped, and he started blubbering again, falling to his knees and pleading with me not to shoot him. I smacked the gun against his forehead, gave him a real hefty kick in the balls, hopefully busting them, and then knocked him out cold with the butt of my gun. I looked at him, sprawled on the ground, and a vicious rage overtook me again. I grabbed his coat hem and wrapped it around the gun to muffle the shot as I placed the barrel to the back of his head, my finger on the trigger. I looked around to see whether anybody was there. I couldn't see a soul.

I still shiver when I think of it. Quite why I de-cocked the gun, I have no idea. I was that close to blowing the miserable little shit to kingdom come. Instead, I holstered the gun and went through the nonce's pockets. I took his keys, got his name, address, date of birth from his driver's licence, took his Social Security card from his wallet, and checked them against the details I'd gotten for the job. I felt some relief when I saw that, yeah, this was my guy. I then put all his stuff into my pocket, I knelt, checked that he was still breathing okay, and then I left him covered there in blood. I rolled the balaclava back up, so it looked like a cap, and put my shades back on. Then I went to recover the tracker, searched his car, took some more personal stuff that might come in handy later, and took off, throwing his car keys down a storm drain.

I now knew I had to report in—or would have to at some stage. I had a long hard think before I made the call. I told the office I'd lost the guy on the interstate in heavy traffic. Then I returned to my position outside his house to await his return—

110

except that I took a book with me this time. I didn't expect him to show for a while, and he never did, so I rang in and said I was finishing for the day.

The next evening I turned on the local TV station and heard on the news that the police had picked the guy up and taken him to hospital. He'd suffered a severe attack at the hands of unknown assailants, it said. He claimed to have been jumped by four guys wearing hoods and robbed of two hundred dollars. They were even asking for any witnesses to come forward.

I switched off, poured a beer, and sat thinking about what had happened. I'd tried to learn to be honest with myself over the years, but even so, it took some time before I was able to admit the truth. It wasn't a bad feeling. The fact was I enjoyed hurting the nonce. I relished inflicting damage on him—even to the point where I almost murdered him, I knew it was hugely unprofessional. Still, instincts had overcome me. I would defend with my dying breath as natural, normal, and human. Could I promise myself it would never happen again? I doubted it. Which begged the question, was I in danger of becoming some kind of vigilante, like the guy portrayed by Charles Bronson in the *Death Wish* series? Yes, there was just such a danger, and the challenge was to try and make sure it didn't happen again. Well, not just yet anyway.

PI Work. (USA) Inga Case.
Messing with the Goods

The previous case was history already. I forgot it had ever taken place. I was busy working on a new case, an ex-nurse, a woman called Inga. She'd been fired from her job by a doctor she worked for, and he claimed she'd been threatening him. She'd worked for him for five years, and it seemed likely that their relationship had been intimate—but the doc said it wasn't, not that we were ever able to prove it at the time. But when you get a woman as pissed off as she was, you have to wonder.

What Inga had done was stole some confidential files from his office. Quite what they contained, he couldn't say, but this was before the days when you stored everything on a computer. We're talking pieces of paper here: names, addresses, private case notes, that kind of thing—and maybe some personal photos and correspondence, because the doc said she'd phoned him a couple of times, threatening to shoot him. But first, she said—or rather, he alleged that she said—she was going to fuck him over by finding evidence that he was having an affair. Not with her, but with some other woman. And then she would reveal all to his wife and family with proof.

The doctor's first response was to go to the police. He got nowhere with them. They couldn't do anything unless or until an actual offence had been committed. If Inga had written a letter, that might constitute evidence of a crime, but a phone call—on his say-so? No chance. The guy obviously thought he was in real danger because he hired a couple of armed bodyguards. Christ knows how much that cost him, but hey, he was a doctor. They're never short of money. The calls from the aggrieved nurse, however, persisted. That's when he wised up, realised he was spending a lot of money for no return and called on us for help.

By this time, he'd started recording the woman's calls. I remember Keith and me sitting in the office, listening to the tapes. The woman was plainly trying to disguise her voice. She sounded like a cheap actor, playing a gangster from a 1930s black and white movie. "I'm not gonna tell ya how long ya got. Just one day, you're gonna feel that bullet rip into ya goddam chest." With the doctor sitting there, pale and trembling, we had a job not to burst out laughing. We told him to give us her number and leave it with us. As soon as he'd gone, Keith called her, and I listened in.

The first thing she asked was, "How did you get my phone number?"

"I got it from a friend of mine," Keith said. "Works at the hospital where a certain doctor has a surgery. A doctor you are acquainted with." Keith gave her the doc's name.

"So what do you want?" she asked.

"Look, it's a delicate matter, but... well; this doctor has been messing around with my wife. And I'm going to teach the guy a lesson he won't forget."

There was a long silence, then she said, "So what do you want from me?"

"Just— er, just a few personal details. Maybe what this doctor does in his leisure time, who he hangs out with. I wanna confront the guy—that's the truth of it."

The woman hesitated again. "I don't know anything," she said. "I mean, I don't even know who you really are."

"Oh right," Keith said. "I tell you what; I'll give you my number. Think it over, and maybe give me a call sometime. How's that sound?"

She didn't sound happy about it—so we were surprised when she called Keith a few days later—and pleased. The fish was on the hook. All we had to do now was reel her in. Keith told her he had a friend—a British guy called Nick Ramayo, who would come over and talk things through with her. According to him, she still sounded wary, but she agreed to the visit. Now it was over to me.

I called her the next day. I put on my poshest British accent, told her I was Nick Ramayo. Nicco for short and asked whether she'd like to meet me for dinner. I told her it would be an excellent relaxing way of getting to know each other.

"Sure," she said.

"Excellent. But look, I don't know my way around town very well. The fact is, I haven't been over here long, so why don't you recommend a place and we'll meet—at what, eight o'clock?"

A woman once told me that I could charm the birds out of the trees when I was on my best behavior. I could hear our nurse relax as she said, "Fine. I'll look forward to it." The English accent works every time.

I showed up early. I had a nice sober suit on, and I arrived in a car I'd rented from the airport. If she was really involved in trying to extort money out of the doc, I imagined she'd be sharp enough to check up on me. I made myself comfortable at the bar, ordered mineral water, and waited. Nine o'clock came, and I was still sitting there like a dummy. Then the barkeep brought me the phone, said there was a call for me. It was Inga. "Something's come up," she said. "A family emergency. Can I take a rain check?"

"Oh, how very disappointing," I said. "Still, these things are sent to try us." Then I settled down to order a meal for one. I might as well enjoy myself and charge it to expenses. Besides, I was by this time starving, not to mention awash with mineral water. I was aware that Inga might well have been watching from the parking lot. I couldn't guarantee it, but it wouldn't have surprised me. I took my time over the meal and left around eleven.

I was busy the next day until mid-evening. I'd just got back to my place when Inga rang. She wanted to know whether we could re-arrange for Friday night. I decided to play it cool and answered, "I'm busy then, but let's see…" I held my diary to the mouthpiece and rustled a few pages. "I'm free on Sunday. Is that any good?"

We met in a bar downtown. I was pleasantly surprised when I saw her. I was expecting some kind of gorilla. The doctor had called her a regular ball-buster, but here she was, about five-seven, with short, neat blonde hair, a curvy figure, and small, delicate hands. I noticed her nails were painted a pale orange colour and the thumbnails bright red, which struck me as unusual. She wore a smart high-neck blouse and a sober grey pinstripe skirt. When she spoke, she spoke with a soft Southern drawl with an accent of some kind. If this had been a social meeting, I would have been interested, for sure.

We got a table, ordered aperitifs, and got down to business. I explained that the woman the doctor was having an affair with was married to a good friend of mine, and I'd volunteered to come over and see whether I could help sort it out as a neutral observer, you might say. I didn't push it, didn't try to explain things any further. I just concentrated on being the Englishman abroad, asking her questions about the American way of life. By the time we got around to dessert, she was relaxed and talking less guardedly. Later she told me where her accent came from as she was born in Scandinavia. When she mentioned that she needed to call a cab to get home, I offered to drive her. I dropped her near her apartment and suggested that we meet up next week, and as I was a stranger in town, maybe she could show me around, maybe go and eat, dance, or go to the theatre. She didn't hesitate. "Sure," she said, "that'd be great."

I went thoroughly prepared this time, with a microphone under my jacket attached to a recorder on my belt. I'd say I went fully equipped, but I wasn't—not for Inga's appearance. She was wearing a slinky dark blue dress, low cut, opaque tights and high-heeled shoes, and heavier makeup and earrings. She looked hot and seemed to be sending out a message. What the hell, I said to myself. All work and no play makes Jack a dull boy. I greeted her warmly, and we ordered a couple of drinks. Once again, she'd come by cab. I was on soft drinks as I was driving.

After half an hour or so, we drove to another bar she wanted to show me. There were music and dancing. She moved damned well. We went to a third-place where we could eat. She started to loosen up, telling me about this doctor, how they had indeed had an affair, but he'd dumped her, and now she was hell-bent on messing him around. She wanted to know what I could do to help. I told her I'd think about it. I said it seemed to me the doc deserved whatever was coming to him.

After we'd eaten, she said, "Has anybody told you before that you are a horn dog?" I looked confused. "Also, I got a few things you might want to take a look at." She gave me a sort of half-smile and added, "Back at my place." Oh shit, I was thinking.

Business and pleasure. It isn't a good mix.

Before we left, I went to the men's room and rearranged my

tape recorder. If the jacket came off—and I hoped it would—I didn't want her seeing that lot. I buttoned the whole caboodle in an inner pocket.

When we got to her apartment, she poured us both a drink. We sat and chatted and had another—and a third. Then she got down on her hands and knees and started to roll back the living-room carpet. There was a sort of under-the-floor closet there. I wondered what the hell she was going to show me—probably the guy's body. I soon relaxed. What she had was the stack of files she'd taken from his office. I looked them over; this was all the evidence I required to solve this case. Not that she'd finished. She also brought up a gun, a .38 caliber revolver, with the serial numbers filed off.

"What's that for?" I asked. She was making me nervous.

"It's only a cheap old thing," she said and laughed. "I bought it off some guy I met. Thought you might need it."

"Me?" I said. "No, thank you. I'm not going to be shooting anybody, and I hate guns."

It seemed that we had concluded the evening's business. But I was wrong. Inga put the gun and files back under the floor and was beckoning me into the bedroom, with her hand held out. I have to say I was taken aback at the speed with which she slipped out of that dress to show her stockings and suspenders. She then undid my pants and dragged me to the bedroom.

I felt uneasy the next morning when I left her apartment; she was a nice and very sexy woman, but this was business, and I made my way straight downtown to the office. I submitted my reports and proof to Keith, who was well pleased. So were the police, who went round to Inga's apartment the same afternoon with a search warrant and arrested her.

Later, as Keith and I relaxed over a coffee and donuts, I

couldn't resist telling him about my conquest. He went absolutely apeshit.

"You what! You fucking screwed her? Why, you dumb fuck, don't you know rule number one? You do not—ever—mess with the goods, you hear me? Jesus Christ! And to think I hired you because you're a Brit. I thought you fuckers were all a bunch of buttoned-up pussies."

When he'd got that lot off his chest, he laid it on the line. If I did that one more time, he would never hire me again under any circumstances. "Have you got that? Have I made myself clear?"

All I could say was, "Yes, boss." I was feeling humiliated and embarrassed, and I was hoping he'd finished. But he hadn't. "Never," he added, "never mess with suspects or clients. If it comes out in court that you've been in the sack, your evidence is—hell, it's a total, instant write-off. And our name will stink. I can't afford to have a bunch of Lotharios on my books. Now, you keep your dick in your pants—ya got that? What you did, it's like—it's like shitting on your own doorstep," he said. "Sooner or later, you'll land in it and fall flat on your dumb ass."

After he left, I breathed a sigh of relief and thought to myself, thank fuck he didn't mention it, or maybe he didn't even know that I was screwing Jolene, his personal secretary in his office, or I would have been toast, but that's another story.

I guess we all need moments like those when we realise we have to stick to specific rules or quit. I determined there and then to get my act together. I resolved that I would try and be professional, and this was a reminder that I had found part of my true vocation in life, so I will have to be prepared to take it seriously. Sure, I loved to screw around, and I did have a fantastic night with Inga; and there were always plenty of hot dates out there, just that I'd now have to leave screwing until after work is finished from here on in.

Party by the Lake

I remember getting invited to go to a party that was by a lake; when I got there, the guests were nearly all drunk. Jonny, whose party it was, was the son of the owner of a bowling alley chain in Washington, which I went to sometimes, to play tenpin and unwind. I met Chevy in there some months before. He was always drunk and aggressive; he thought because his father was rich, owned a few businesses, and was quite well off, he could treat everyone like shit! I had to calm him down on many occasions when he got drunk. Once, I took his car keys from him while intoxicated, with his drunken wife near the car. I had gone over to him as he was struggling to get his keys in the door. "Jonny, let me help you with that," I said and took his keys and threw them in the lake, saying, "Now you will have to get a cab home." He would always threaten to put me in the hospital one day, but never did, and the next day, he would apologise to me. He was apparently still beating up his wife when he was drunk; she always had black eyes or bruises on her face.

I always wore my Kevlar vest under my shirt even when I socialised, and today was no exception. I had my .38 revolver strapped to my ankle and Sig Sauer 9mm in my belt. I went over to the grill, grabbed a burger and a soda, and was chatting to some girls when I heard a scream and Jonny shouting. I went round the back of the camper van and saw Jonny slapping his wife around the head. I ran over and barged him in the chest, knocking him to the ground, and shouted, "Pick on a man that can fight you back, you fucking coward!" He got up and picked up an empty bottle, and smashed it, and came at me, waving it like a knife. Now a lot of people were standing around, watching, and no one wanted to get involved. I was blocking his moves using my martial arts training. I knocked the bottle from his hand and caught him with a punch to the side of his face, causing him to spit blood. He fell hard to the floor, knocked out for a few seconds.

All this time, his wife was screaming and shouting, "No! Don't hurt him!" As he lay dazed on the floor, I offered him my hand to pull him back up. With that, he wiped the blood from his chin with the back of his hand and shouted, "I'm going to get my gun, and fucking kill you, you motherfucker!" and ran to his camper van. I shouted as he ran, "Don't come at me with your gun in your hand Jonny, you know I won't hesitate to shoot you!" His wife continued to scream, "No, Jonny, someone stop him!" She ran inside the camper van. I had to assume he was getting his gun, and I knew he carried a .45 cal. Smith & Wesson.

How the hell does an alcoholic get a licence to carry a gun? I thought to myself. I pulled out my Sig from my waist holster, checking one round was in the chamber and aimed my pistol with both hands, with the gun cocked and pointing to the camper, waiting to take the shot if he came out with a gun. I shouted to Jonny, "Come out of the van and let me see your hands!" By this time, some friends had also run into the van. I stood there, poised, at the ready, controlling my breathing. Then I heard a shout, "Ted, please don't shoot, he's coming out, and he hasn't got a gun!" I saw his friends come out first, pulling Jonny with them, with all their hands raised to their shoulders, no sign of any guns. I was still standing, poised with my pistol cocked. Then I shouted to his wife that she had better come out too with her hands up!

"Everybody keep your hands where I can see them." I could

hear his friends standing around saying, "This is bullshit, man, it's a party," but I was also aware that they knew I had a bad reputation for shooting people dead without warning. You never know when the wife will stick up for her husband, and she might have decided to take the gun and shoot me instead. She came out with her hands to her head. I then scanned my weapon and looked around to make sure none of his friends had a gun to use. Then I thanked them for their invite and slowly walked backwards towards my car. I was saying to them all, "No one makes any sudden movements towards me while I drive away, please. You all know I have a very itchy trigger finger." I slowly got into my car, still with my gun, scanning my audience, and put my key in the ignition to start it up. I wound down my electric window and jumped into the driver's seat with my pistol now held out of the window with my left hand and still scanning my audience with my right hand on the steering wheel. I wheel spun my car out of there, throwing rocks and dust about as I gained distance. I fired off a couple of shots in the air and shouted, "Yee-ha!" and left the area. I drove for a while, checking in my mirror for signs of anyone following me with guns, and eventually, I holstered my weapon. I started to sing along to the radio and thought that this is another day in paradise for me. For some reason, I never got another invite to any of his parties after that.

The Bodybuilder Incident

I had the authorisation to pick up two guys on bail, but their court date wasn't due for at least another two months. Both of them shared an apartment and were regular bodybuilders. They were both built like brick shithouses and pumped up with the help of steroids. Both were out on bail on drug charges, and there was a warning on their rap sheets that they previously carried firearms. And as a precautionary measure that day, I took another Taser with me as a backup, as I knew I could not shoot these guys as they may not have guns on them while on bail. But I knew they would give me a load of aggro being pumped up steroid junkies. Also, as I was working on my own, it would not be easy to independently cuff both of them.

I managed to get a backup guy to come with me. We had a tip-off that the guys were training at a gym and the address. The tip came from an ex-girlfriend of one of the guys, she had posted bail for both of them, but she had recently caught her boyfriend round the back of the gym having sex with a female staff. She decided the only way for payback was to have his arse thrown back in jail until his court date, so she gave the bonding company the tip-off, stating that she wanted to come off the bail bond, which meant we had to put their asses back in jail even though they had not missed their court date yet.

We arrived at the gym and parked in the car park. I walked over to the gym and sneaked a peek through the glass window, and could see the two guys we were after pumping weights. They were bigger than I thought. I was told by the bonding company that they had additional charges, which were added later for threatening witnesses in the hope that their cases would be thrown out of court when they appeared. When I saw the number of bodybuilders in the gym training with them, I decided to wait until they came out. I saw on the bonding information sheet that when one of the guys was bonded out, he owned a red Chevrolet Camaro with a beige leather interior and used it as security on the bond. We saw the Chevy in the car park and waited near it, calling up the recovery truck to repossess it, but none were available. About two hours passed, I had already noticed the gang graffiti on the walls, which read 'Blood 7th Street Gang Area'. I had been in this area before and knew the gangs operated here, as I had previously arrested here before.

About 11 p.m., when the car park security lamps were on, the two guys emerged from the gym; no one else came out with them; both came walking out carrying their gym bags. They headed towards their car. I told the other agent to stay in the vehicle and only shoot if I ran into trouble. I ran to their car before they got to it. I was in full uniform, and I had a Taser in each hand. I shouted to them both to stop and put their hands up, that they were under arrest, and I was taking them both back to jail. I had the two red Taser dots positioned on their chests. They shouted some abuse at me, then threw their bags down and charged at me. I fired off the two Tasers, hitting both of them in the chest; they both crashed to the floor and were shaking like they were having a fit, waving about their hands and feet.

I would normally only press the trigger for six seconds, but it felt like I pushed it for a lot longer, like double the time! I shouted to the other agent to quickly get the handcuffs and zip ties out, as they were coming round far too quickly. Each time there was any sign of movement from them, I pressed the trigger again and again. What seemed like to be minutes were only a few seconds. Eventually, we cuffed them both up hands and feet and then hogtied them both.

That was the least of our problems. Given our truck's size, we tried but couldn't even lift one of them into the back of our vehicle. So we had to dial 911 and ask for police backup, as both these guys started to recover then started shouting for help, hoping that their friends would come out of the gym to back them up. As well as not being able to lift them, we worried about all the other gym people starting on us. Even though we could draw our weapons, we would not be able to shoot them. Thinking quickly, I ran to my truck's back and got a roll of duct tape and a couple of cloths. I stuffed the fabrics in their mouth and put three duct tape layers around their heads to shut them up.

At last, they were silent, murmuring on the floor. And about twenty minutes later, two police cruiser trucks arrived for backup and helped us carry the prisoners into their cruisers, and I took the Chevy key from one's pocket. I would have to come back for the Chevy later if no recovery was available. I then rang again for the recovery truck, which came 15 minutes later, and had the Chevy transported to our storage yard as bond collateral. Then at least, this would cover some of my costs to the bondsman. I then rang the guys' ex-girlfriend and told her that both were in custody, and she would now be off the bond as soon as she had gone to the bail bonding office and paid our expenses and recovery fees in full, which she wasn't very pleased about!

Homeless Hobo Trap

I remember one very old case in Seattle I worked on; I had a tip-off that the skip I was after stayed with a friend in a tower block in Pine Street, Seattle; very near Pike fish market. The tip-off had told us that the skip had been seen going in the building a couple of times. The trouble was that I could not park my car nearby as it would get towed away, and I did not know which apartment number the skip was staying in. The front desk had a security guard, but unless I knew which apartment he lived in, I could not attempt to enter it, just in case the guard warned the owner of the apartment I was on my way up. So I had to come up with a new idea.

The next morning I went to the local thrift store after thinking and sleeping on it for the night. A thrift store is where you can buy washed second-hand clothes; the money made goes to various local charities. The trouble was they looked too clean, so I bought them, then drove down to some muddy wood, tied them on a rope to the back of my truck, and drove around with them on tow for about fifteen minutes; I then took them home to dry them out after smearing some black used oil over the coat and hat. When they dried, I put them on and looked in the mirror. Fantastic, I thought. Now I looked like a real bum that lives on the street, and I made up a cardboard plaque that said 'Hungry, Thirsty, Homeless and Broke—PLEASE HELP ME—Thank You God Bless you. — Bob xxx'.

With that in hand, I put on my black uniform early the next

morning and put my dirty old clothes over the top of it. I carried an old dirty blanket to sit on, and an old plastic bag with food and water, plus a McDonald's pop cup, and strapped my gun to my hip, and headed off to sit outside the building in Pine Street to wait. I was also wearing an old cowboy hat to protect me from the sun. I found a spot outside the building in the shade, placed the blanket down, sat down, and placed the pop cup in front of me with about $5 in loose change inside it, to stop the cup from blowing away. I put the cardboard plaque on my knees and waited.

About four or five hours passed, people were passing by and throwing loose change into the cup, and without looking up, I would say, "God bless you," all the time watching who came in and out of the building. A couple of cops passed by and ignored me when I asked for spare change. About twenty minutes later, a taxi pulled up outside, and my skip came out with a young lady. I jumped up, threw my old coat and hat off, showing my uniform shirt, quickly drew my 9mm pistol, and shouted, "Freeze, motherfucker, bail enforcement hands up!" He immediately obeyed without any hesitation, his young girlfriend started screaming, and someone called the cops. I had already holstered my pistol and cuffed him and was about to call the cops myself when they screeched up with guns drawn on me. After I showed them the warrant and my ID, they had to laugh, saying, "You must be that crazy limey bounty hunter they are all talking about."

"Yes, sir, that would be me!" I laughed. "Could you two officers help me out and book this guy into your jail and sign my warrant?"

"Sure," they said after I shook their hands. When I saw the police cruiser pull away, I went back to my begging place, picked up all the gear and placed it into the bag, and took a big swig of the tepid water from the bottle I had inside. People were stopping and staring at me with their mouths open, chatting with each other. Maybe they thought I was an undercover cop or something? I grabbed my begging cup and counted how much was in there— Wow! –Fifty-two bucks! Now it was time to buy a free lunch and beer and go to pick up my $2000 reward. Not bad, $2,052 for a day's work, begging.

***

A Few of my Secrets / Bounty Hunter Fees.
    I would put my job percentages as follows:
70% – Boredom
20% – Excitement
10% – Terror
'Courage / It's being scared to death, but going anyway.'

***

When the bonding company calls in the bounty hunter to find someone, the bondsman is already in a losing position. His defendant has already skipped bail, and he doesn't want to pay out of his profit any large finder fee's to the bounty hunter. On the other hand, he doesn't want to lose 'good graces' with his insurance company who backs the insured bail bond. If he has too many defendants on the run, he will lose face with the courts, and in the end, his bonding business will lose money, and he will be bankrupt.

    Sometimes, a bail bond company has already gone bankrupt with having too many skips that failed to appear (FTA'd, as they say in the States). What this means is the skips are still on the run. The forfeiture bond still has to be paid to the courts, even though the bonding company has closed down. The insurance company that backs the bond will still have to pay this money fully to the courts as they guaranteed the bond. So to recover some of the insurance company's money paid to the court, the insurance company will also hire bounty hunters to go out and find these skips to recover some of their money back. They will put up reward posters, in shops, newspapers, etc., just like the old Wild West days, when a sheriff hammered a couple of nails, using the butt of his pistol, into wanted posters. Open to anyone that can help bring this wanted person in for a reward.

Needless to say, bounty hunting is not a soft occupation. It is dangerous work, as the job is to track and subdue hardcore criminals. At times lethal physical force must be used to bring the skip back to custody. The actual tracing process involves one of the most challenging kinds of traces there is. The bounty hunter often has to deal with the hardest career criminal elements, involved in drugs, stolen merchandise, murder, and prostitution. Tracing such persons involves the criminal side of the law, unlike most private investigations, which deal with the law's civil side. However, with good skills, huge rewards await them on the felons' recovery for those daring enough to try it.

So, if the standard basic bounty hunter fees are 10% plus expenses, if a bond is set at $100,000, then the bounty hunter will get a $10,000 finder's fee, plus costs. But the finder's fees are not cut and dry; bail bonds can involve considerable funds if the bond had been set at $250,000, even $1,000,000, so if the skip is not found, the bondsman stands to lose the $250,000 or $1,000,000 to pay to the court. It could put him out of business as all his profit has gone, as I've said previously!

The very basic finder's fee for the bounty hunter is 10%. Some bonding companies will not pay expenses; it has to be negotiated at the time of the contract before they start hunting the skip down, and the bounty hunters won't get paid anything unless they bring in the skip before the police find them. The difference with me was that I was a well-established bounty hunter, with a high success rate of tracking and arresting. I would continuously work at recovering the skips; I was a workaholic, and I loved the work. So one day, I thought, why should I just accept the basic 10% commission on a recovery?

When I got called in, I would tell them if you want to pay the standard 10% recovery fee, call in any novice bounty hunter and sit and pray and lose sleep that they bring him in before the bond is forfeited!

Or pay me a retainer for costs incurred and a commission of 20% plus expenses on the skip's recovery, and you can then sit back and relax, knowing I will almost 95% guarantee to get them and bring them in before the bond is forfeited. Just look at my track record with other bonding companies. And of course, I would agree to return the retainer in full if I failed to bring the skip in, but I have never failed and never had to refund a retainer in all the years I have been doing recovery.

Remember, bounty hunters only get paid when they find the skip and bring him in. They won't get paid unless the skip is caught, arrested, and placed in custody. If they don't find the skip, all the money they spent trying to locate him is their loss, which means if the cops get him first, we get nothing!

Deal with Crooked Cops

There was a case that happened some time ago that I remember very well. The bounty hunters did a deal with some of the local crooked cops in New Jersey. As the cops arrested the skips, they would check and see if there was a bail bond on them, then if so, they would falsify the arrest forms as though the bounty hunters had made the arrests; this way, the bonding company would have to pay out the reward, and the hunters would split it with the cops. In the end, they got caught, lost their jobs, and all went to prison.

Another case I read about concerned a group of bounty hunters who went looking for the violent skip on the run with a considerable bounty on his head. The bounty hunters got sloppy and desperate. They did not check where, and if the information they were getting was correct, they got a tip-off by phone giving the location where this skip was hiding out. They all raided the house late one night, breaking in the door, searching the house, and held all the people living there at gunpoint, only to find themselves all being arrested and charged with felony charges. All because they got lazy and did not check out who was giving them the information, and then checking to see who lived at the property before breaking in the door. The house they raided was only the home of the chief of police.

First, I would check with the police and jails that the skip hasn't been picked up locally or anywhere in the United States. Remember, bounty hunters have the same access to information as the police have access to use, as we all go after the same individuals on the run. We can check personal records, rental company records, traffic tickets, vehicle registrations and then see what the bondsman has obtained collateral, i.e., cars, boats, bikes, jewellery, guns, houses, etc. And I would also pick up the collateral, bring it back to the bondsman's storage place, and log it all in. The items brought in would help the bondsman recoup my retaining fee.

Many novice bounty hunters start to look for defendants that have skipped bail, but of course, they will have to use their own money for costs until they find the skip. If they can't find the skip, they can't reclaim their expenses. Many novice bounty hunters will bullshit the bondsman that they are frequently still out looking for the skip but haven't found them yet. They cannot afford to lose any more money or time tracking them down. To be successful, you have to have money in the bank and take risks. I always updated the bondsman, so they knew I was still on the case.

Most parents, who pledge property and goods as security for their son, daughter, or relative, fear the consequences if the person they posted bond for is not brought in before their court date. The bounty hunters will call, and the co-signer will lose property, cars, boats, and even their home! I know bonding companies with lists of homes they repossessed, which they keep for rent or sell to recover their costs; it's a booming and profitable business. When a guarantor agrees to write the bond and takes the cash commission, he will also take deeds to a real-estate property, car titles, boat titles. He will get the documents notarized to ensure that other items like jewellery, guns, etc., belong to the bonding company. Most bail bond companies have a public notary working in their office to endorse and secure the bail bond.

So now problems have begun for the bondsman. He has lost

contact with the defendant. A bondsman also list houses and places their defendant must stay while on a bail bond, as they are now his prisoner and must inform him where and when they are going anywhere. So the skip or defendant has also failed to phone in regularly to the bondsman's office, and also the bondsman will call them regularly to make sure his bail bond is secure and to remind them of the date he or she has to go to court. When the defendant is released from jail on the bail bond, there are specific rules set they must adhere to.

Remember, they are on bail instead of being held in jail until their court case. The bondsman is now like his prison officer and must keep an eye on him. They must not leave the state, carry any weapons, and regularly contact the bondsman.

Picking Up Skips Without Warrants

When I track down a wanted person who has skipped their court appearance, I am not just tracking down one skip. I could have as many as fifty to sixty warrants in my files. Sometimes, I would use a pinboard that sat on my passenger seat, with photographs of skips pinned on it. You never know when you are going to pass or recognise a skip when driving through the streets. It also helps to have all the warrants with you.

If I drive through the streets and I recognize a skip, and I may not be on contract to pick that skip up. I would first check the system and make sure there was still a warrant out for that person; only then do I arrest without a contract, but not before first checking who wrote the bail bond and contact the bondsman; if the bondsman agrees to pay me, I will arrest them without a warrant.

I have done this many times, and when I have captured the skip, I would either get a bondsman to meet me at the jail or I would drive to the receiving bonding company to collect the warrant, but only after they assured me that I would be paid the bounty on the skip. Even though I have no contract with this particular bonding company, they will pay me the reward. As they would also have other bounty hunters looking for the skip, and they will be glad to have the skip locked up and are free from the bond.

When the skip is locked up, this will mean they won't forfeit the cheque held at court for the defendant, and they will keep their cash deposit. I may also pick up some collateral to cover my costs from the person that guaranteed the bail bond.

Bounty hunters can find bonded out skip cases by checking civil records, such as indexes in county court-houses. The skip tracers will always find several instances where the courts have filed a forfeiture notice against the bail bondsman and insurance company for bond forfeiture. In one instance, you can locate several dozen cases in less than one hour. If you call the bonding company and no one calls you back, or you have not heard anything from the companies about these cases, it means you will not get paid if you pick up these skips; therefore, it's not worth arresting them. If the bonding company does call you back and agrees to pay you, you can agree on a fee plus expenses.

Temporary cells in Bonding Offices.

In some bonding offices, they have their own prison cells. At my recovery office, I also had two cells, with their own beds, toilets, washbasins, like open rooms, but with bars across one side with a door. Sometimes, I would crash out and sleep in there myself. These cells come in handy if the bounty hunter has picked up a skip and the police cells are full, which they are most of the time, or the warrant is out of state, and he cannot be transported there and then. When this happens, the only problem is that someone has to stay and watch them all night, feed and give them water, and keep an eye on their well-being, and it's usually the bounty hunter who has to do this. It is a bit like in the old western films, when you see a deputy or the sheriff sitting outside the cell with a Winchester rifle, keeping guard on the prisoner.

Now the bondsman realises the defendant has skipped, and he has not appeared for court, and he has received a forfeiture notice from the court. The court will give the bondsman a time to bring the skip back or lose the bail amount. It may be thirty to sixty days or could be longer, but it is usually a date and at midnight that day, miss this date and time, and the bondsman is expected to pay the full bail amount to the court, i.e., $100,000.

The bondsman can hope that the police will stop the skip on a routine stop or something else and bring them back as the warrant will be on their system. But remember, the police do not have the money or resources to spend on hunting wanted people and tracking down criminals. If the police arrest the skip, it hasn't cost the bondsman a cent, and there is no commission to pay the bounty hunter! Remember that local, State police, federal marshals, and the FBI also hunt fugitives, but a bounty hunter's financial incentive often leads to faster apprehension. In other words, bounty hunters are far quicker at finding and bringing skips in, but they need paying.

But what if the police don't find the skip? The police are not going to trace and look specifically for the skip, even though it's registered on the police system, and there is a warrant for the skip's arrest. It's just on their system, and it will be just pure luck if they pick them up on a routine stop. If they do, the bondsman will have saved his fee that he could have paid to the bounty hunter—but if the skip still is wanted, then he must pay the $100,000 to the court on the final day, and now it's too late. The court has taken the bond, and with a few more like this and the bondsman goes bust.

Bonding companies need bounty hunters, and sometimes, they are desperate when a person has skipped bail. They will employ anybody who walks into their office with a good sales pitch. These so-called bounty hunters are wannabe's that seem to misunderstand the experience needed and the dangers involved in doing this job. Facts show this is why so many novice bounty hunters get killed—about 50%.

One thing the bondsman doesn't need is a novice bounty hunter going out after his skip, with no training and no insurance, kicking in doors, or maybe killing the skip or the wrong person. If a parent gets killed or the bounty hunter is killed himself, the bondsman risks getting sued for damages, but some desperate bondsman will use them anyway.

Most professional skip tracers or bounty hunters will have a good track record, which the bondsman can call other bonding companies to check his story. Most bounty hunters will have their own insurance and full experience of the law and their powers of arrest. Remember, if a defendant has skipped bail, finding them isn't going to be easy, as they know the law is after them, and they have now committed another offence of bail jumping, failing to appear, etc.

Although there are many professional bonding companies in the industry, quite a few have bought the industry into disrepute to hire bounty hunters, which are thugs and seedy characters with no licence or insurance. When a defendant has skipped bail, some hire criminals, believing it 'takes a criminal to find a criminal.'

When someone skips their bond, they can be tracked anywhere in the United States because, at the time they signed for bail, the defendant signed away any rights they had, which includes being re-arrested by the bondsman. After posting bail and taking the 10% cash fee, the bondsman can, at any time, arrest and put the defendant back in jail. If the defendant continues to break the law while on bail or becomes a flight risk, they will jeopardise the bond being forfeited in full by the court. Putting a defendant back in jail under these circumstances is a sound judgement by the bondsman, and the Indemnitor (the co-signer of the bond) will still lose the 10% cash fee.

Although this court decision has long been established, it is sometimes often misunderstood, and it seems police officers still do not fully understand the law in which bounty hunters work. They hate it when a bounty hunter tells them the law and quotes the Supreme Court ruling or show them what law he works under. The police always have to check with their superiors before the officer intervenes, and he breaks the law.

Things That Go on in Police Custody

I've seen and witnessed vulnerable women that have been arrested and placed in the cells, where correction, immigration, and police officers have forced them to have sex for cigarettes, candy, food, or even make telephone calls. When you are arrested and searched, they place your money, jewellery, etc., in brown or manilla envelopes to give you back when you are released! Sometimes the money, jewellery, and personal possessions disappear when they are arrested and placed into custody. They are sometimes too traumatised, drunk, or high on drugs to check and sign for their property. Sometimes personal stuff seems to disappear, but trying to press charges against an officer is virtually impossible.

My Nightmares

When I returned from the States, I suffered from terrible nightmares every night, and I still do this day. It was like I had pushed all the hurt and violence deep into the back of my mind and had forgotten it ever took place. But it was always there lurking somewhere deep in my subconscious thoughts, even though I never thought of it while awake and doing normal everyday things. I realised that violent films and small incidents would trigger them off. I found myself sometimes waking up in a cold sweat at night; I did not know where I was, if it was real or if I was still dreaming.

Sometimes I thought I was still in the States; I would wake up and walk around the house, but I was still asleep; I would see gang members all around me with guns and knives, stabbing and attacking me. I would start coughing and choking, as I thought they had cut my throat, I would hit out in my sleep, and it was a job to break out of it. I didn't know how to control or stop it. Sometimes I was sure it was really happening, and it was taking place there and then. The dreams were so very vivid; the people threatening me looked like they were real people.

When I met my wife, Irena, I told her everything about what I had been through in the states; she was terrified of my nightmares. She said I would shout out for help, and she would shake and shake me for ages; sometimes, I still had my eyes wide open, and she would think I was dead; it would take a long time to break me out of this sleeping nightmare. She was terrified that

I might kill her without realising what I was doing. Sometimes I would even go and sleep in a different room and lock the door because even I was terrified of what I might do in my sleeping nightmares. I always had the fear that I might think that what was really happening to me, and I might fight back or end up killing someone. When they checked me out, the doctors felt it might be better to section me; I refused to tell them the truth about my past, and I knew why this was happening. They would never understand or believe the things I have done and had to do. Nowadays, it's like two or three times a month I get these nightmares, but they are still there lurking deep in my subconscious mind. Now I know they are not real, and I am dreaming, but I always shout for my wife to wake me up when it happens.

It went on for many years, I thought they would never go away, but now they have gotten more infrequent. At one stage, it used to happen in the daytime if I had a nap. They were the scariest things I have ever seen or been through; they go beyond the imagination. Sometimes I would even think I was going mad or crazy and losing my mind. Because of all the things I was doing in my work line, including shooting people at close range, I knew it might affect me one day. I realised that when I was tracking dangerous skips, I knew I would kill them, and I may get killed myself. If people knew what was going on in my mind at the time, they would think I was crazy. Many doctors in the UK were still totally unaware of the *[17]MAOA gene, later I found out I had a problem, and the results showed there was no known cure for it.

---

[17] * see glossary

C.J Johnson—Bail Bonds

Sometimes when I was out tracking skips, I would pop into other bonding companies that I did work for, even though I was not on contract to work on their bonds. They would still look up the files and help me with additional information and addresses they had, as most had bonded the same person out on bond at some time, and data would still be on their system.

One particular time, I think it was about 3 a.m. but still night (Bonding companies are open twenty-four hours). I had gone in to see the manager, Ron of C.J Johnson bail bonds in Tacoma, just to check if he had any further data on his system on a skip I was tracking that morning. I leaned across the front desk with my hands clasped together, and Ron was explaining a few things, along with some general chit chat. He must have been showing me something as he was waving his hands in the air. I had a black MA1 bomber jacket on, but my pistol may have showed tucked into my waistband at my back as I was leaning across the desk.

As my back was facing the outside window, Ron noticed many police cars passing by without light on; I glanced around and carried on chatting to Ron. I then went behind the desk to collect some printouts he had printed for me; I said goodbye and started to walk out of the front door. As it was very dark, I did not see two police officers at the sides with guns drawn. I suddenly became aware of something and went to grab my gun. All these spotlights came on when all hell broke loose, and blue and red lights started flashing. The police had surrounded the building, jumped on me with guns blazing, and threw me to the floor. I hadn't a clue what was going on, and they took me by surprise. Ron came running out, shouting what the hell is going on, and informing them that I was a Federal bail agent. The police spoke to Ron, and I showed them my ID. They un-cuffed me and handed back my weapons, explaining that a concerned citizen was driving past the bonding company and thought I had a pistol pointed at Ron and his hands were up and felt that I was robbing the place, so the police came in force, as I was armed. I did find it a bit funny and shook all the cops' hands when they apologised to me, but I thanked them for getting there quickly and not shooting me as it could have been Ron getting robbed or even shot. It wasn't amusing at the time, but each time I met Ron, we would always bring it up and have a laugh; it could have ended badly, but luckily it didn't.

Press and TV

I found out by chance that I was attracting a lot of unwanted press attention, as newspapers in the States were starting to mention me by my real name and where I came from. I remember getting off a plane from Seattle to Heathrow airport and seeing a lot of press waiting for someone with cameras ready. I thought there might have been a celebrity behind me, only to find they were waiting for me!

At first, it was great to be like some sort of film star, but I started to wonder if this new-found fame and publicity that I was getting would now put my life even more at risk in the States.

But I went on to do many television talk shows and series, here in the UK and the USA. I also did a series in the States called '*Bounty Hunters*,' which went out on *Channel 22*—I think we shot about sixty episodes. Most got shown in the TV series. I also went on to do many TV chat shows and editorials for well-known magazines and tabloid newspapers worldwide.

But I could not talk or even mention anything about the classified undercover work I was doing for the FBI.

Bounty Hunter Ride-along Course

After being fully keyed up on tracking skips down for rewards, I had a great idea to give the general public a taste of how it all works in the States.

In 1998, I started to offer a unique vacation. I likened it to a safari hunting holiday, like hunting big game, except hunting wanted armed people! People would apply to come and join me on the bounty hunter ride-a-longs, making arrests and having their photographs taken with prisoners before they were taken to jail. I was already doing it when I trained new bounty hunters, or I had various business people that I worked for that wanted to ride-a-long and see precisely how we track down skips.

It took off pretty well, I had lists of people wanting to do it, even with the bad publicity it got, and it caused quite a stink in the UK Parliament. I had British MP's writing and calling me and the American police asking me to reconsider it; I was overwhelmed with calls from the national press and TV companies wanting to come to the States and film it with a big-money offer. My phone was constantly ringing, but I would not allow any filming for public television, no matter how much they offered to pay me. Yet, in the end, the US authorities admitted that there was nothing they could do to stop me, as I had the licence, insurance, and gun authorisations in place. There was nothing the American authorities could do unless they passed a new law to ban me.

Ted-Cam Incident.
Hungarian Girl

Izabella was a young nineteen-year-old Hungarian girl, who I met working as a waitress in Pegasus Restaurant in downtown Tacoma, Washington. We were filming the '*Bounty Hunter*' series at the time, and the team and I used to go there for breakfast before we started filming. Izzy was the waitress that served at our regular table, and I got on very well with her; she told me she was engaged to an American guy, but they did not live together. When I went into the restaurant, I was always wearing skin-tight, light blue jeans. American guys usually wore baggy blue jeans and checked cowboy shirts; she kept telling me that she knew I wasn't from here, as I was different from all other guys that she had met. She said she could not take her eyes off my tight bulging jeans that I wore each time I came into the restaurant; Izzy said it made her get hot and flustered.

I was surprised when Izzy asked me out on a dinner date. Even though she was a beauty to look at, I would never have asked her out in a million years, and she had mentioned that she was engaged to be married soon, leaving me even more surprised when the dinner date was going to be at her flat, and she was cooking. I asked if her boyfriend knew I was going there; Izzy assured me that he didn't know anything, and it was nothing to do with him what she did in her own private time. Also, he never came to her place without calling her first, and he was working nights that week. I wasn't sure what to expect, so I agreed to go to hers for dinner. Of course, after we had a very romantic dinner with plenty of flirting, she excused herself and later came out of the bedroom in a short white see-through baby doll nightie with nothing on underneath, so I stayed all night, why wouldn't I? I started taking her out on dates whenever I could, or if I went back to the UK for a short break, she would always call me on the phone and then meet me on my return, and we would go to lunch then back to hers for sexual fun. Once, I arranged to meet up with Jolene for brunch, the blonde investigator who was also the secretary of Keith Taylor from the Investigation Company. I was dating her on and off, and Izzy turned up in the restaurant; out of the blue, Jolene got very jealous. It turned into a full-blown row in front of the other diners. It was very awkward; I paid the tab and walked out.

One night us and the film crew, all men, were all sitting in a bar/restaurant in downtown Tacoma having a few beers, laughing, cracking jokes, and looking at the days filming on the camera crews' monitor that they had brought into the restaurant to watch and check. We had to make sure it was okay to put on the '*Bounty Hunter*' series, which was running weekly on the American TV network *Channel 22*. When my cell phone rang, it was Izzy asking if she could come and see me. I told her that I couldn't see her tonight or the rest of the week, as we would be going out filming again later for the TV series, and I was on a tight schedule, and that we were with the TV crew right now, checking the day's filming. She asked if I was with other girls as she could hear women laughing in the background; I told her I wasn't with any women, and those she could hear were in the other bar; it was all men I was with. She said she felt a bit jealous and needed to see me right now as she needed to talk to me tonight. I told her I couldn't leave the crew, as we planned on going out again. She asked where I was, and I told her I couldn't tell her that, as it was a secret location and that we were in a restaurant/bar's private room at the back. She kept saying she needed to see me right this minute. I told her I would call her later in the week. I then switched off my cell phone and got back to enjoying my evening with all the lads.

Concealed in my uniform, I wore a miniature camera and microphone attached to my bulletproof vest, giving a point of view film action as it happened. Which the film crew called the 'Ted-cam.' About an hour or so later, into the room walked Izzy with a big grin on her face, having found me. She later said that she drove around Tacoma, looking in all the bars until she spotted my truck in the car park. She came in through the bar in a micro miniskirt, not leaving anything to the imagination and a see-through top. Everyone was giving her wolf whistles as she walked through the main bar to the back. She asked if we could go somewhere private to talk. I excused myself from the lads and took her out the back door to the car park to save her from the embarrassment of walking through the busy main public bar again. We went and sat inside my truck.

She went on to talk and said she was jealous of me being in the private bar and me refusing to meet up, and then she went on to tell me she was deeply in love with me. I told her that I liked her a lot and loved being with her, but I didn't feel the same way, and I did not want a regular girlfriend in my line of work. We started to kiss, and it went on to heavy petting, and to cut a long story short, we had oral and then full sex on the back seat of my truck. I didn't take my clothes off, only dropped my trousers, just in case we got called to go on the road with a crew, after we finished sex, I suddenly realised that the 'Ted cam and microphone' was switched on. In our moments of passion, I had accidentally knocked the toggle switch to the 'on' position. Izzy panicked and said, "Oh no! Please tell me It wasn't on and filming us having sex?"

"No! Of course not, I only just knocked it on," I said.

I had quickly switched it off. I told Izzy I would think and discuss what she felt about me later next week, and I will then decide where we will take our relationship. She got in her car and left, refusing to go back to the restaurant/bar as she was too embarrassed as my buddies may have been watching us having sex.

I walked back into the bar-room to find all the film crew and my lads all smiling, sipping their drinks and whistling, and they quickly switched the monitor off. I said, "for fucks sake, you dirty bastards, you weren't watching us, were you?"

"No, of course not, 'BOHICA[18],' one shouted. "Yes! Harder, harder, Oh! Oh! I love you, Teddy!" They all laughed and admitted they watched the whole thing, but they all had their eyes covered up on the rude bits! But I made the crew delete the film in front of me. They said it was better than watching a 'point of view' hardcore porn movie.

---

[18] See Glossary

Rolling Meth Lab Case

The rolling meth lab is a mobile laboratory used for the illegal production of methamphetamine. They are very hard to detect when moving, and many are only accidentally discovered by police stumbling onto them or K9 dogs picking up the scent, which smells like urine. Also, the chemicals used in the process are very poisonous, inflammable, and highly explosive. They use stolen vehicles for this process because the substances used impregnate and coat any vehicle's interior with its toxic residue, rendering the vehicle virtually worthless and contaminated.

These illegal labs are often driven to a secluded location by road. As the dangerous, strong toxic fumes they give off can easily be detected in a residential area. So they make the drugs in the back of stolen vans, trucks, or even eighteen-wheeler lorries while on the move. This way, empty toxic waste drums can be thrown out into the forest areas while moving.

I was with a film crew on this particular case, as I had a tip-off from a snitch that our skips were hiding in some densely wooded area in a large camper van; the snitch had drawn a map of how to get there and told us they were making drugs in the truck and selling them while on the move. Again I agreed with the snitch, a down payment, and a balance when I arrested the skips. We headed out at 2 a.m., while it was still dark and quiet. I had three other bail agents with me. All dressed in full black uniform, night-vision goggles, respirators for chemical usage, a backpack full of small white flags on sticks, etc. Before we packed and left our office, everyone was given instructions on what our hand signals meant we would use and what they must do if we came across any booby traps. Also, no one would talk on this mission until the skips were cuffed and arrested. Everyone needed to be fully aware of all instructions for safety.

We parked our vehicles off the main road on a dirt track and headed to the location, walking to the area where the skips were supposed to be hiding with their rolling meth lab.

The other agents and I had night vision goggles on. We tied a rope around each other, including the film crew, as we had to walk in a single line for safety; We knew there would be hidden booby traps set up around these rolling labs, and we all needed to look out for tripwires. After about twenty or thirty minutes, we arrived near the location, and we spotted tripwires around the hideout with the night vision goggles on. We passed the message down the line that a booby trap was in front, and I placed a few flags from my backpack, either side of the tripwires. There were quite a few traps set, I had told the camera crew they could film, but no lights could be on. At each end of the booby trap is a flashbang or explosive filled with shrapnel that will go off, maiming us and warning them that someone is approaching, and they may flee or start shooting at us.

When we arrived at the location where the skips were hiding, there was one large trailer and two Dodge vans. You could smell the ammonia wafting in. I signalled that everyone should stop and put on their respirators. As we got nearer to the vehicles, we undid the rope, and we left two agents with the camera crew. Rob and I went on forward, towards the vans. I had to give the signal to stop suddenly, as in the night vision; I spotted a long lead with a dog asleep at the other end, under the van. I quietly put the silencer on my gun; I would have to shoot the dog, but as I aimed, the dog got up very slowly, looked around, fell and staggered, and fell over again, then went back to sleep. I realised the dog had been sniffing the drugs all day and was also under the chemicals' influence. I had also told the camera crew that as soon as I had the skips under control, they could light the place up and film everything. I would set the booby traps off after I arrest them; I would then have to call the police and [19]hazmat team, as I didn't want the police getting injured on the booby traps getting to the location.

As I got nearer, I waved up all the guys in the team; we had previously planned the hit on paper as to who was doing what. I had no other choice but to shoot the dog first just in case it came to and attacked us when we grabbed their owners. Then we crashed in, with flashlights on our weapons, and within minutes it was all under control, with no shots fired. We had four guys cuffed up and two girls, including our two skips, lots of drugs, money, and illegal guns, including an AK47[20]. We called the police, as they would arrest them and charge them all. I let the film crew light the place up, and we got them to film everything for evidence before the police arrived. We set off some of the booby traps that were farthest away from the rolling meth lab. As there was less risk of an explosion due to the chemicals and fumes, we left the booby traps near the meth lab marked with white flags. We placed many extra flags around them, so no one accidentally set them off. I sent one of our team to the road to help bring the police and hazmat team in. The place was lit up with searchlights from the helicopters overhead when the police arrived, and I told police that I did not want the press to interview us, as I knew they were on their way, but agreed to be at the station to make statements in the morning. It was a significant police bust on television! We were never mentioned.

---

[19] See glossary
[20] See glossary

Thanksgiving Day Arrests.
Breaking into Houses and Deadly Force

Thanksgiving is a Federal holiday in the USA. It is usually on the fourth Thursday in November. Each Thanksgiving Day was a speciality of mine, and I travelled to different states each year for the usual surprised round-ups.

Almost everything closes on this memorable holiday. Public transport is limited. It is a day that families and friends get together for that special family meal, turkey, stuffing, potatoes, and pumpkin pie, etc.—like we have on Christmas Day.

Americans go really big on this popular time, to take time out and travel the distance to celebrate with all the family. Before Thanksgiving Day, I had already contacted quite a few bonding companies to see if they had any cases that the bonds were about to be forfeited for FTA. I always managed to get about thirty to forty urgent arrest cases. These were ranging from $10,000 to $200,000 bail bonds, which the defendant failed to appear on their court date.

Now the bonding companies who put up the bail bonds were required the pay the defendants' outstanding bail amount in full to the courts. The arrest warrants were all around the state of Washington, which made it a lot easier to do. Most of the bonding companies were closing up for the break, but some still had a skeleton staff on standby. With most staff working from home, they would answer the phones, write the bail bonds, and then deliver them to court.

Sometimes, I would deliver the bonds myself to jail and get the defendant to sign the paperwork. I did this to make personal contact with the defendant; then, if they jumped bail, I was 100% sure of who I was going after.

It wasn't usually busy over this holiday period. Nearly all the bonding companies told me to do these after Thanksgiving, but I said to them that Thanksgiving was the best time to round them all up, as I had done this in many states in previous years, and it was very successful. I would also tell almost all of the bondsman that I am British. We do not celebrate Thanksgiving Day. It's a badass job, but somebody must be thick-skinned to do it, like a British bounty hunter.

I only take long breaks when there are no skips to find, and that's not very often. Most of the skips will go to their parents' homes after they have missed a court date, and they will always be there on Thanksgiving, as most of the parents' family homes are where they are supposed to be while they are on a bail bond.

Remember, unlike police officers, a bounty hunter does not need a warrant to enter a residence if they think the defendant may be at the home or any other place listed on the bail contract.

Why?

When a defendant is released on bail, it means that the state allows a person who would otherwise be in jail to go free under certain conditions, pending his or her trial.

American courts' traditional view is that the state continues to have the same power over an accused prisoner, whether or not they are released on bail. In order to secure their release on bail, the accused has to sign a contract that gives broad powers to the bondsman, and if a person jumps bail and fails to appear in court, the state or its agents (bondsman) have the same power that they would have over an escaping convict.

Another point when a bounty hunter breaks and enters a house, a third party may think this is breaking and entering as we are not police officers. They may use deadly force to stop us from getting in, as most Americans have guns at home and will use them without hesitation if you are in or on their property.

There is a common-law rule that allows a person to avoid a conviction for homicide if they killed another person to defend their home. Lawyers call this the 'castle defence,' and it's based on the idea that a man's home is his castle. That rule still exists today in the US. But in general, the use of deadly force is only justifiable when a person forces entry into a house under circumstances that suggest that the person breaking in is about to kill or inflict serious injury on one of the inhabitants of the house, or the person is at least about to commit a serious felony.

Under this rule, it's unlikely that any US court would ever find that it was justifiable to use deadly force against a bounty hunter who is only doing their job. After all, even if a bounty hunter mistakenly breaks into the house of a third party, their intention was to simply apprehend a fugitive, not to commit a felony[21] or harm the inhabitants of the house. So remember, if a bounty hunter breaks into your home, you may ask them to leave; if they refuse, as most times we will, you may call the police. You may even use 'deadly sarcasm' against the bounty hunter. But you cannot use 'deadly force.' When entering a person's residence, we would always be dressed in full uniform, carrying sub-machine guns and pistols in case of a shoot-out.

I went to the gun range the next day, practised my shooting skills, and then did a bit of karate training; then after a few beers and a hot-tub, I went to a barbeque with some of the other bounty

---

[21] See glossary

hunters and a few females, we all had a lot of stories to tell and laugh about on our day out. I would always tell people about when we broke down the door and searched a house, to find no one home after a search. We thought the skip had escaped, so we had all holstered our guns, we had cleared the house as safe.

I went to the kitchen fridge to see if I could find a cold drink, as it was a scorching hot day, and my mouth was parched. As I pulled open the fridge door, I had the shock of my life. The skip was inside the refrigerator sitting on a stool; it had a handle inside to open it and a gap at the back for air! He could have easily shot me if he had a gun. After that, I always checked and opened the fridge with my weapon drawn when I did house searches. Some people would still laugh and ask me why I always looked in the refrigerator for a skip?

That was why!

I also knew that I would be getting a lot more work coming my way the next year because of all the arrests we had done on Thanksgiving Day.

Bring on the next Thanksgiving Day.

'It's Eight, not Six Stupid.'
FBI taught me this in Training

Remember, for each case I work on, 90% is a lot of paperwork, surveillance, long stake-outs, tracking, bribing, telephone calls, door knocking, speaking to friends and family of the skip, ringing police precincts to see if they have picked up the skip. The last 10% is the thrill of making the arrest and can be the most terrifying part of it.

It was a scorching hot day, and I had to take the morning off to get some groceries in, get odds and ends done, such as replacing ammo, car repairs, etc. I made the stupid mistake of taking off my bulletproof vest and throwing it on the back seat, as it was a scorcher that day. I still had my model 627, Smith & Wesson snub-nosed .357 magnum revolver in a holster on my waistband, with a sleeveless shirt over my pants, hiding it.

I forgot you could never have a day off on this job. After calling to see if they could fit me in, I headed down to the auto shop to get my Bronco 4x4 air-conditioning recharged and sorted out, as it was not blowing icy cold but warm air.

I took a short cut to the auto shop, as it would save me twenty minutes. I should have avoided taking the downtown gang-banging area route, but I was running late. Pulling up at the stoplight, signalling to turn left, I became aware that I was the only car on the road. I also became aware of a beaten-up ragtop (convertible) blue sedan pulling out of a side street, with two black males inside it; they followed me along the deserted road, which had few houses dotted about here and there.

They pulled up right behind me, also signalling to turn left; I could see them both talking in my rear-view mirror; they were discussing my truck in front of them, possibly recognizing it from previous arrests I had done in this area. I suddenly saw an Uzi sub-machine pistol being cocked in the passenger's hand and a gun in the driver's hand! Fuck, they were getting ready to ambush me!

I quickly accelerated through the red light, turning left with a cloud of burning rubber and squealing of tires on the hot road. There was a burst of machine-gun fire hitting the rear and back window, blowing it out. They also hit my front and rear tire, which caused my truck to skid and crash into a ditch across the road, ending up almost on its side but only tilted. I undid my seat belt and quickly scrambled out, as they had started to open fire again. I hid behind the engine block and front wheels of my truck. I pulled out my revolver and returned fire, firing three shots into the side of their car, missing them but smashing the side windows. They were now outside, hiding behind their car. My truck was fucked and hissing steam from the radiator from where it had bullet holes.

They shouted to come out, and they would not shoot me; they only wanted to talk. Like fuck would I ever believe that. Both fired again, and I fired off three more shots, skimming and hitting one of them in the shoulder. I checked my revolver—two bullets left, none left in my shorts pocket to reload.

I remembered my training and I had an idea!

It just might save my life. I moved the two bullets past the hammer on the pistol, stopped on the third empty chamber, and closed the revolving chamber.

Again they fired at me, and I stood up and clicked off four

157

empty shots and pretended to look at the empty gun in shock. They both started to laugh out very loud, and they stood up and were reloading their weapons as they walked towards me. I was still standing up facing them, with my pistol pointed in their direction. I clicked off two more empty rounds—click! Click!—and pretended to shake with fear. They laughed out very loud now, almost crying with laughter and slapping their hands together in a high five. As soon as they were in close range, I aimed and fired off the two remaining bullets, hitting both of them in the chest and knocking them both off their feet, with the power of the .357 magnum bullets whacking hard into their chests. Their guns flew from their hands as they fell hard on the road. I walked up carefully and picked up their Glock pistol, checked it was loaded, and then picked up the Uzi machine pistol, and I stared at their very shocked and surprised look on their faces, as they struggled to hold back the blood pumping from their chests, "How?" one chokes, and spits out blood in disbelief.

"It's an eight-shot pistol, not a six-shot, stupid!" I replied with a big beaming grin on my face.

The best bit about this situation, it paid off. Later I found out that the two gangsters were both wanted on warrants, and I got paid to shoot them, covering the costs to repair my truck.

Timothy Taylor
A Case of a False Hand

Again, I was out doing personal stuff on this particular day and was in plain regular clothes, not in uniform. It was later on in the year, near Thanksgiving Day. It was freezing, actually icy cold and snowing. I had my overcoat, bulletproof vest, leather gloves on; my badge hung hidden around my neck and my pistol on my hip. When you are out and not working, you never know who you will recognise and bump into. You might see someone who has a warrant out against them, and a day of shopping can turn into a lucrative payday, like this day.

I was shopping at a store when I spotted a guy with his gal shopping inside. His face looked familiar, so I went back out to my truck parked outside near the shop and checked my warrants, keeping an eye on the store in case they came out. I flicked through the files of warrants, my breath steaming from my mouth like puffs of smoke. Boy, it was bitterly cold! At last, I came across an old case I had, but I could never find him. Timothy Taylor wanted for 'assault and battery' and domestic violence. No firearm warning on his rap sheet, but you never know if he's got an illegal gun. His bail was only $15,000, but that would give me a reward of 20%, that's $3000 in shopping money to spend, if it is him, I thought. As Taylor's case was an old case, I thought I'd better check in with police warrants first to make sure it's still on the system and active. Quickly, I dialled the warrants department, always watching my suspects shopping inside the store.

They confirmed it was still an active arrest warrant, but the photo was old on my file. The guy looked similar to him in the shop. Could it be his brother or a double? Firstly, I had to be 100% sure it was him. I can't go pulling a gun and make threats to shoot him, and it's the wrong guy—I would get arrested and sued!

I had to come up with an idea, so I quickly looked in the back of my truck to see what I could use. As I was rummaging through my gear, I came across my tailor's dummy, I had an idea, and I took the right arm off the mannequin. Those readers are more interested in what I was doing with a tailor's dummy in the back of my truck. Professional bounty hunters put these in uniform and keep them sitting in the truck to look as if we have backup when we are really on our own, with an option on dodging fines in the fast lanes as laws state you are supposed to have more than one passenger in your car to use the fast lanes.

I placed the dummy's moveable arm in the front of my truck and waited until they came out of the store. After about fifteen minutes, they came out, carrying lots of shopping bags, and got into a truck opposite me on the other side of the road, laughing and kissing. I noted the make and licence plate.

Silver Dodge Ram Truck, licence plate: DRE 547.

Then I rang in the plate to the police to see who owned the truck. It came back as registered to a 'Virginia Ryan.' It could be his gal, I thought, but at least now I have an address to work on.

A few minutes later, the truck started up and pulled out. I started my truck and followed with a blanket car in front of me. I will have to jump a few traffic lights if needed, I thought.

Slowly, it got dark, and eventually, the truck pulled onto the drive it was registered to on the system, and the loving couple got the shopping out and went inside the house. I parked a little further up the road with my lights off. I had waited long enough, as thirty minutes had passed.

If this was my guy, this is why we lost trace of him. He is living out in the boonies (remote area) with his girlfriend, whom we knew nothing about. Or is it the wrong guy? I had to find out as there was $3000 waving goodbye to me if it was him, and I didn't check it out.

I took off my overcoat, placed the false arm inside the right sleeve, put my glove on the hand part, and secured it against dropping out. After doing up all the coat buttons, I then got out of my truck and pulled the overcoat over my head. It was an oversized overcoat with plenty of room inside. I pulled the other glove onto my left hand and wrapped a scarf around my neck; I then held my false hand with my left hand in front of me just below my waist. I kept a sheet of folded paper with my left thumb and false hand—a photocopy of the warrant, in case he tried to grab or tear it up. I took my snub-nose pistol out of its ankle holster with my right hand and held it forward in the ready to fire position inside of the coat, aiming in front. I looked at myself in my truck mirror to make sure it looked okay; I looked a bit fat but averaged looking. I then headed to the house.

As I got to the door, I pressed the bell with my chin. There was a loud bell 'brriiinng,' and I stepped back away from the door. A few seconds later, Virginia came to the door and asked if she could help me. "My name is Dan, and could I have a few words with Timothy Taylor, please? I know he is home," I said, a big smile across my face.

"Um! Um!" she mumbled.

"It's okay, I will wait, as it's very important."

"What's it about?" she asked.

"It's one of a personal matter," I stated in my best English accent.

I heard mumbling behind the door, and the guy came out holding a black pump-action shotgun, aiming it in my direction. He told his gal, "Get inside now, bitch."

"Could you not point that thing at me please, Mr. Taylor?" I stated. "As you can see, I am of no threat to you and unarmed."

"What do you fucking want, dickhead?" he shouted at me.

"I have a warrant for your arrest, Mr. Timothy Taylor, and with your co-operation, I would like you to accompany me immediately to the local police precinct so that I can book you into a holding cell."

He started to laugh out loud.

"Ha! Ha! Ha! Ha! Ha!"

Glancing at my hands, which were still holding a piece of paper in front of me, as he again aimed the shotgun at me, yelling, "Get off my fucking property now or I will shoot you where you stand, you stupid son of a bitch!" Just as he went to pump a shell into the chamber—Bang! Bang! Bang! I fired off three shots from my hidden snub-nosed revolver under my coat, hitting him in the chest and arm, immediately causing him to drop the shotgun and fall back against the door and into the house. His girlfriend came out, screaming and crying, "You've killed him!" I let go of my false hand but still held my pistol in my right hand, quickly undid the buttons on my coat with my left hand, and threw my coat onto the ground. They could now see my vest and my badge hanging from my neck. Timmy was screaming in pain, and I shouted. "You stupid —fucking idiot!" I then asked the girl if anyone else was in the house and then pulled out my cell phone. I kept my pistol pointing at them both and called for the police and paramedics, stating, "Emergency federal bail agent serving a warrant. Suspect shot but still alive." I cuffed them both up, then applied a tourniquet to stop the bleeding. Within minutes, the police and paramedics arrived. I put my gun down, complied with the orders the cops were giving me, and lay spread-eagled on the ground in the snow until they checked me out and allowed me to stand, and gave me my weapons back. Now I would have to go down the police precinct to make a statement as the skip would now have another charge against him of firearm offences. After it was all over, I rang in the warrant so I could get my paycheque. I looked at my all-wool overcoat with three fucking bullet holes in it, well I thought, I will use part of the $3000 to buy a new coat, but the arm! Very handy, very handy indeed!

When doing close protection work, federal agents use this false hand technique—holding one false arm in their jacket with one hand and holding a gun inside a coat with their other hand, saving time not having to draw their weapon if there is a threat.

Bail Bondsman/Rude Incident

Most bail bonding companies will pay up straight away after you have put the skip in jail and saved their insurance bond, but there are always one or two crooked shady ones that make some excuse and won't pay you, and you have to keep calling into their office. They are never there for you to collect your hard-earned bounty and expenses.

A bondsman named Chris owed me money and was avoiding me. The payment was eight weeks overdue, and every time I called him or went to his office, he would be out and would never return my telephone calls. I found out that he liked to party hard, and I heard Chris was continuously going into table-dancing clubs. I knew many girlfriends who worked at these clubs for some extra income; some were also doing sexual favours' for cash. I had previously told a friend of mine called Trisha about Chris owing me a lot of money, I gave her a photograph of him and told her if she came across him to call me so that I could get my payback, and there would be a big cash reward of $5,000 in it for her. It would still be cheaper to pay her than trying to drag his ass into court.

One night a few weeks later, I got a call from Trisha and her friend Debbie, telling me that this guy Chris, had been in their club and had taken them back to his private flat that night for some sexual fun. Funny, I thought, this guy is married with kids. Trisha told me they had got his wallet and ID and realized this was the guy who owed me some big bucks.

He was drunk as a skunk and drugged up, and they told me to come over and bring my video recorder and camera with me.

When I got there, Chris was lying naked across the sofa arm, with his hands tied up, with a large black dildo rammed up and sticking out of his ass. The girls stripped naked and stood over him, doing all sorts of nasty sexual things to him, while I clicked off lots of photographs, then I videoed the whole thing. The girls were wearing masks to cover their faces. The girls took the $800 in his wallet for their services. After we all left the flat together, I told them that if I got all my money back, they would get the $5000 reward.

Later, I sort of blackmailed Chris by posting copies of the photo's to his office, saying, pay up plus my interest, or these photos and video will go public and to all his family members!

Guess what? He paid in full and the extra Interest I requested for taking so long to pay me, no questions asked, and he made no threats. Of course, I gave him the originals after he had paid up. I didn't really want to embarrass him in front of his family. The girls got their $5K in cash, and I never worked for this crooked bail bondsman ever again.

The Ex DEA Agent

I rarely worked with people I didn't like, and the only time I did, was when a bondsman that I dealt with regularly asked me to help them out on an urgent case. I had to work on one occasion with one of their bounty hunters named 'Tim Mannion.' He turned out to be a pathetic, big-headed show-off. Before he started at the bond company, he was a DEA agent. He got caught holding a stash of drugs and money that the DEA had recovered from a drug bust. They knew one of their team was dirty, so they set a trap, and he walked right into it and got caught. He was arrested but never charged and was also dismissed from the DEA.

On this particular day, we had gone out and tracked down the skip, arrested the skip, and transported him to the local police cells, but I could not find anywhere to park my truck near the police precinct. So I dropped Tim and the skip off on the corner while I drove around and looked for a parking bay. The skip was handcuffed behind his back, and I had put shackles on his ankles so he could not run away. I had to go back around the block again while still looking for a place to park; I passed Tim walking behind our shackled skip with his weapon drawn and pushing the skip in the back with it, as the skip shuffled along the pavement to the police station. He had this big 'Look at me. Look how tough I am!' expression on his face, as everyone stopped and stared. My truck came to a screeching halt in the middle of the road, and I flew out of the truck and went fucking mad at him! I shouted, "Put that fucking gun away! He is not going to run anywhere, you stupid fucking asshole!" He ignored me and went into the police precinct. I eventually found a parking bay, and I went into the police cells; I apologised to the skip before he was put into the cells saying, "Excuse my partner, he's a bigheaded asshole for the way you were treated."

The skip replied, "Thanks, man, no problem." It ended up after the skip was booked in with a full-blown row outside the police station, with us pushing and shoving each other. I told him that I do not humiliate my prisoners, and the next time I saw him pointing a gun in their backs, I would draw my weapon and fucking shoot him in the back. As he came to get back into my truck, it had just started to pour down with heavy rain. I knew he didn't have a car and had no cash on him. I just locked the doors of my truck, locking him out, wound down the electric window, and said, "Fucking walk back, Mr. Ex-DEA agent! You fucking bigheaded asshole, you're never going to work with me again!" and drove off, leaving him standing there in the pouring rain with only a shirt on. I told the bondman I would never work with that big-headed dickhead again. And I never did work again with Mr. Ex-DEA Fucking Asshole!

Crooked Bounty Hunters

One other small note, there are a lot of dodgy and untrustworthy bounty hunters out there. I remember when we were doing the 'Bounty Hunter' series for television, this was one arrest that we backed up another bounty hunter called Robbo for the show. I knew Robbo from previous back up arrests I had helped him on; he was always stone broke and living day to day, hocking all his stuff to live on. We were hunting a guy called Jarvis Cobbe and had come across the shack late one evening, where we had been the tip-off that he was hiding. We kicked in the door and went in with guns blazing, catching our skip off guard and arresting him. There were a few guys and a couple of partly clothed girls with him. We checked out the girls and the guys for warrants, but they were given the all-clear, so we told them to leave the property before the cops got here. When we searched the property, we found a box full of cash and wads from his drug dealing business. As we were still filming all this for the show, we left the money where we found it, telling our skip that we were only interested in arresting him for the bail bond company and not reporting him to the cops as to where he got all this money from. We fixed the lock on the door and locked it as best we could, then we took him to jail. On our way out of the police precinct after booking the skip in, Robbo stated he must have dropped his new flashlight where we made the arrest, and he needed to go back and look for it.

As we were in separate cars, the film crew and I became suspicious, and we covertly followed him back to the property to see what he was up to. We waited near the property, hidden with the camera running. Very strange that he had parked his car a block away from the property. We then saw him pull on his gloves then knock on the door. As no one answered, he then drew his gun and kicked the door in again.

Breaking back into the house, knowing that the person is not there now becomes a criminal offence, as it's breaking and entering. He spent less than five minutes in the property looking for this supposing lost flashlight. We watched as he came out of the property and pulled the door shut, holding his hand inside his jacket, wondering if it was the cash he was really after. Whether he got the money or not, we will never know, as he failed to keep in touch with us and moved house.

Native American Territory

While working in different States, I always seemed to pick up warrants to arrest quite a few Native Americans. Today I had a warrant to bring in one called Johnny Jerome. Most of the time, when I went onto these reservations, I had to obtain the help and permission to enter tribal land from the tribal police that police these reservations.

When you look at the statistics, crime remains an endemic problem on Native American tribal land, with shocking homicide rates, skyrocketing levels of juvenile crime, gang activity, child abuse, and substance abuse plaguing the over 1.4 million people populate the tribal lands. Crime rates showed that Indian and Alaska natives' violent victimization is 2.5 times greater than that of other ethnic-racial subgroups within the United States.

I obtained the nickname of 'Black Raven' from the Chief of the Cherokee tribe reservation. He told me he gave me that name as I seemed to swoop down from the sky and suddenly steal one of his people. Whenever I was passing the reservation, I would stop by with a bottle of Jack Daniels Whiskey, which the Chief and I would sit and drink together and have a pow-wow. (Meet, celebrate, dance, socialize, and honour their cultures).

I did have a lot of sympathy for the Native Americans. It was their land. Through the years, the Americans had carried out some terrible massacres from the 1539 Napituca Massacre to the 1890 Wounded Knee Massacre when the 7th Cavalry killed 250 Sioux men, women, and children.

The Native Americans who live on these reservations live in appalling poverty and slum conditions. Yes, their reservations are tax-free, but that's about all the American government gives them for free.

Let's go back to Johnny Jerome. I went onto the reservation to arrest him, and as they say, nothing is worse than trying to capture a drunk Red Indian. He put up one hell of a fight, which ended in me getting covered in mud all over my uniform. But I managed to cuff him to my wrist and took him into the police cells. When I got through the booking process, the police came out to take the prisoner into custody, and they almost took me as I was so dirty with mud, they thought that Johnny was the bounty hunter.

UK and USA Police.
Tasers, Guns, Training, Smuggling, Statistics and Facts

While working in the states, in addition to my guns, I always carried an X26 Taser. First, you have to attend and pass a "CEW" (Conducted Electrical Weapon) Master Certification Course. The pass at the end of the course allows you to carry a Taser and is valid for two years. The course was a five-day training course, which was a written and practical exam. (which the British police do not have to do). To complete the test in the final part, they tell you to take your shirt off, and two guys stand either side of you on a padded floor to cushion your fall, as the final part of the test requires that you have to shot with the taser in the back. Two guys hold your arms; they tell you to close your mouth with your teeth clenched, as you might bite your tongue off when the Taser darts hit you. They shout, Taser! Taser! Taser! Then, fire the Taser into your back, and believe me, the pain is excruciating like a vast electrical current has invaded your body, you cannot move, and every muscle in your body locks up. Anyone that has been shot by an electronic control weapon will experience neuromuscular incapacitation.

Another significant point they teach you on the training course is that you must never discharge a "CEW" when gasoline, gases, fumes, vapours, materials, or other flammable liquids are present, as this can result in a fire or explosion.

There were a couple of cases involving British police with Tasers in the UK, which I read about in the papers.

Maybe the British police instructors don't teach about these dangers when using a Taser, or if they do, the police are not all listening to what the risks are, hoping that they will never have to use the weapon.

The police had arrived at one incident, in which a guy had just tipped petrol over himself and was threatening to commit suicide. He was going set himself alight with a cigarette lighter. The local police arrived armed with Tasers, and one cop tried to stop him from committing suicide by firing his Taser at the guy. When the Taser darts hit, they ignited the fuel vapour. They helped the poor guy kill himself in a ball of flames.

When you fire a Taser, inside the cartridge are between 20-30 small pieces of confetti-like tags, which are ejected from the weapon when deployed. These are called AFID's (Anti-Felon Identification Discs). On each of these AFID's is printed a coded serial number, which allows the police to determine precisely which Taser cartridge was deployed and to whom it was booked out. When I spoke to a friend who is a UK firearms officer about these AFID's, he said he had never heard of them. Very strange!

***

The second incident was the Raoul Moat case in 2010. Moat had been on the run for almost a week; after shooting three people with a sawn-off shotgun, the police eventually contained moat in an open field. when he stood up, he aimed the gun at his head, threatening to kill himself, stating 'it ends here.'

I was surprised to hear that the police had used the new X12 shotgun and its "XREP" shells for the first time in the UK (Which stands for Extended Range Electronic Projectile). The X12 shotgun fires a twelve-gauge wireless XREP projectile and has a firing range of 100 feet; the XREP can be discharged from any standard or pump-action shotgun. Later, they made the X12 shotgun in yellow trim, so it would be easier to tell which weapon held the lethal or non-lethal rounds. As soon as the electronic slug is discharged from the gun, it speeds through the air with its four sharpened electrodes and will penetrate the suspect's skin and causes sudden muscle paralysis.

When the X12 came into production in the States in 2008, I went on the manufactures training course just after they went on sale. I was very interested in what this weapon was capable of doing and thought it might be useful in my weapon collection.

For example, when you have multiple targets to control, correctional officers, facing the worst-case scenario—a full-blown prison riot or crowd control. The 20 seconds of voltage emission when the XREP slug hits its target allows the officer's time to close the distance to the subject and restrain them. It's a must-have non-lethal weapon with a more extended range than the X26 standard Taser. If you use the pump-action shotgun, you can fire off all the XREP shells by pumping the gun to stun multiple targets.

Remember that stun guns have been limited since their birth; you had to be close and make contact with the subject, so has the Taser, by its length of wires and barbs, if you miss the target, you had to reload, which takes time, putting you at risk.

When the police used the X12, not one but two of them, for the first time on Moat, I was surprised to hear and see it was being used in the UK, one year after its production. Which was still undergoing testing and had not yet been approved for use in the UK. The officers used it without any training. Yet! When they used the X12 on that fateful day, the police stated that the officers were aiming the experimental X12 shotgun, both fired the weapon at Moat's chest. One missed the target, the one that hit Moat said, "Moat let out a noise as if he had been struck by something. He then rocked back slowly and discharged his shotgun; they could not be sure if the XREP shell hitting him caused him to discharge the shotgun, or he deliberately pulled the trigger to kill himself? I know what I believe happened, as I trained with this weapon, and the subject will lose all control when hit with the XREP slug. Later, a spokesman for Taser International in Arizona said the company is no longer "actively marketing" the X12 shotguns or their electronic XREP ammunition due to low sales. However, you can still buy the X12 and XREP slugs in the States today.

There were just over 123,000 police officers in England and Wales at the end of March 2018, and only about 5% of them were firearms authorised.

When you look at the statistics, authorised police firearms officers in the UK only undergo an initial 15-week course. At the end of each week, a qualification shoot is based on the tactics taught that week. Fail the qualification, and you're on your way home. The attrition rate is high, and rightly so. At the end of the course, there is an exam/exercise that encompasses multi-disciplines learned during the course. They must also pass their final qualification shoots for all weapons. They must also pass their fitness test and specialist Tac-Med course, where the officer is taught how to try and save the life of the person they have just shot.

I also once showed a friend, a British firearm cop, how to disarm a man at close range using my close quarter training. He stated it was impossible with their high degree of training. I proved it was not impossible by testing it on him three or four times, showing how easily I could grab his gun or break his trigger finger with no effort. He said that the police had never taught him this.

In the States, most police officers must practice shooting about twice a year, averaging less than 15 hours annually. Most of these officers revealed that they practiced on average 24 times a year with their own handguns.

In contrast to my frequency of training in the States, I had to train weekly, sometimes daily, as the chances of a shootout were daily occurrences.

To this day, I still go five or six times a year overseas to shoot. It's not cheap and can cost from £1,500 to £4,000 for the course, as live firearm training and ammo are extremely expensive. These regularly shooting courses I attend are always fully booked; most people on these courses are ex-military or mercenaries. And the courses are not just standing on a shooting range and firing at stationary targets—these are full combat situations, including drills for malfunctions, decoking and reloading with either hand, etc.

You can attend these courses anywhere abroad, like Poland, Lithuania, Latvia, and in all surrounding EU countries. You can't even go out with a water pistol in the UK as the police panic and think it looks like a real firearm, and you risk getting arrested or shot. The best bit about shooting weapons overseas is that you can still fire any weapon, auto or semi-auto, including .50 caliber long-range sniper rifles.

Another important tip is to plan to practice at least twice a week if you go to a gun range to shoot. You do not need to fire off hundreds of rounds of ammo, as ammo is costly. Shoot at least fifty rounds at each shooting session, but make sure that every shot counts, fire every shot as if it was the only round left in the gun, and you need to hit your target to save your life. It would help if you always clean your gun immediately after use, especially if you are using corrosive ammunition or the firearm has been exposed to water, moisture, or other damaging elements.

But when you look at the comparison, the chances of an armed incident in the UK is still scarce, compared to the USA, where it is a daily occurrence. But even with our strict gun laws here in the UK, police and border officials struggle to stop a rising supply of illegal firearms being smuggled into Britain. The increasing supply of guns results from dishonest UK border security, corrupt staff, and organized crime gang innovations.

Smugglers have increasingly found new ways and innovative routes to get guns past border defences. When we had open borders, it was also challenging for our police and border force to check everything that comes through the ferry ports, and the criminal gangs from Russia, Romania, Bulgaria, Poland, etc. They think this is a risk worth taking. They sell them to the underworld and any member of the general public that will pay the price.

For example, a Yugoslavian or Romanian AK47 rifle with fifteen rounds in the magazine will cost between £1,000 to £1,500. If you want a Sniper rifle with sights, that will cost £2,500. Illegal trafficking in small arms and light weapons is estimated to be worth between $1.7 to $3.5 billion a year to criminal gangs. You can even buy hand grenades, rocket-propelled grenades, and mines if the price is right.

Where are all these weapons coming from, you may ask? Firstly, you need to look beyond the mountains of the Balkans. And across the vast, remote forests in Eastern Europe, networks of criminal gangs have access to millions of weapons that have been cached after years of conflict or are in general supply in the areas bordering the conflict zones, such as Ukraine.

Also, if you have the basic knowledge and some essential equipment and a lathe, it's straightforward to adapt a blank-firing and deactivated gun, which is still legal to buy in the UK. And these, too, are bought legally by organised crime gangs in Europe who then 'reactivate' them—often by removing an obstruction from the barrel—and sell them onto the criminal market.

The (NCA) National Crime Agency, the British version of the American FBI, will maybe find one or two illegal gun hauls out of about eight that get through into the UK. But to be quite honest, the NCA is working hard and solving a lot more crime than the police do.

It's also a well-known fact that in the UK today that the police do not investigate the most severe crimes anymore. With as much as 9 out of 10 serious crimes going unsolved, they just get written off to make their outstanding crime figures look low. Knife related crime recordings are sky-high. It didn't help when the metropolitan police announced new guidelines designed to screen out thousands of crimes without any investigation, great news for the career criminals! Nowadays, you can dial for an emergency, hoping the police will come to your aid. They might not arrive or even make contact with you for 2-5 days in some cases.

So one may ask, why do I still regularly pay and go to all these firearms training courses? It's no good to rely on the British police to come to your aid in an emergency or a civil riot. You have to be prepared and stay one step ahead of them and take care of yourself, especially when you see that crime is no longer being investigated properly. They say it's because they don't have the funds and the officers to investigate all the crimes committed anymore. The police and government now prioritise covid fines, online hate crime, protecting mosques, and the increased revenue from speeding fines. Somehow thousands of police officers are suddenly found for the easy targets, but none are available to solve a real crime. The figures show that most serious get written off. At the end of 2017, police forces were accused of deliberately targeting motorists to raise revenues after it emerged they received an extra £12 million from speed awareness courses. It's still going on now.

At the end of 2019, figures showed that speed awareness courses have soared in the past few years, with police forces now pulling in more than £50 million annually from these schemes. Yet, the police still state that they are underfunded to investigate all serious crimes committed. Even rape has now been decriminalised, and investigating underage white child sex abuse, no chance of that, as the police fear being accused of racial prejudice—what a pathetic country we have become.

Most of us have lost all respect for the British police. Some lie on statements so they will get a result from a guilty plea at court. A couple of times, I have been to court and proved that the police made a false statement. I even looked in one of their officer's notebook at court. I realised the notes were wrong, and when the judge dismissed the case at court, I said to the judge that the officer lied on oath. But the judge refused to do anything about it. It seems that the police are exempt from being convicted for perjury. Only we can be condemned and get two years in prison.

Look at the 'Covid 19' lockdown. Only essential workers were allowed to leave home, and yet there were three times as many police speed camera vans on the road, catching the easy targets, motorists. Why couldn't they use this valuable time, when we were all on lockdown, to concentrate on solving some severe crimes instead of increasing their revenue from motorists and 'Covid 19' fines? You now see as many as 6-8 police officers turn up at your home to fine or arrest you for not wearing a mask, out walking, or having too many people in your home. Pathetic! Not many people have any faith or trust in the police in the UK anymore.

I was once so proud of the UK, its laws, and our British police, but now it's all gone downhill, and we are a laughing stock to the rest of the world, look at the referendum to leave the EU; I have never felt so ashamed of my country. It took over four and a half years to leave because of our bias court Judges, House of Lords, and MPs; They did not want us to leave as they were earning big backhanders from the EU. Hence why it took millions of British people to vote for Brexit. It has shown us all what a pathetic bunch of clowns we have running our country, and it was fuck what the British people think or voted for. All of them pocketing big expense claims and wasting our hard-earned taxpaying money.

The British police have really lost the plot; they have certainly lost the streets; all you see now is our police running away from violent ethnic demonstrations, getting down on one knee. But if you are demonstrating peacefully and are the British public or veterans, it's riot shields and batons. It's a two-tier policing. What happened to the oath police swear to protect the public? They don't anymore. One day the people will turn the tables on the police. Once upon a time, you would never dream of assaulting a police officer; that doesn't count anymore as they are not our police anymore. Most are our enemies.

But look back at these *[22]snowflake demonstrators who were

---

[22] * See Glossary

threatening civil war, they haven't got the bottle to take on any real action, they don't even know what a real bloody battle is, but they certainly will when we battle-trained old school join together in retaliation and go into battle with them. There will defiantly be a lot of bloodshed and bodies on the street. It will be a massacre.

And it also seems that the only type of people applying for police careers now are the timid cowards that were bullied at school. They get that uniform on and feel powerful; they hide behind uniforms and warrant cards. They certainly love to bully the public and throw their weight around. It's all ego. But in the end, they are still cowards when you get them on their own. Believe me; I should know, been there done that got the teeshirt.

Maybe, later on, I should write a few books on the police nonces and corruption, as I've got enough names and proof. And when you look at the *National Statistics, there were 1771 deaths in 30 years in England and Wales from people being in contact with the police, either in custody or otherwise, with no media coverage, and zero officers convicted. Even the CPS are distorting the truth at courts to secure a conviction.

There are millions of us, and if we all stick together, we can't lose, as we outnumber the army and the police. Our forefathers fought and died for this country, so we could all have our freedom, so we must fight back or become enslaved to a future controlling government and a police state.

Let's hope that the UK will one day become the great nation it once was. A country the world looked up to. Instead of an embarrassment, we have become. (First rant over)

---

* https://www.inquest.org.uk/deaths-in-police-custody
https://policeconduct.gov.uk/deaths during or following police contact

Stolen Bikes
(Leagrave, Luton)

I remember my son and his friends' bikes getting stolen some years back when they were young. They were playing football in the local leagrave park. The bikes had locks and harden steel chains on them; they were cut with a bolt cutter and stolen. It was a Sunday afternoon. I called the police, but they said they were short-staffed and could not send anyone for at least two hours; I told them I would look for them myself. My sons informed me that all their friends had put the theft on social media. So I went looking for the bikes myself without the help of the extremely busy police. Later, some local kids stopped me and told me that they had seen some gypsy adults riding the two bikes at the park's back near where they were stolen from. I went to the parked caravan site and, as there was only one road in and out, I blocked the road with my car, called the police again, and told them that I had located the bikes and where I was. They had better get here quick as there would be a violent breach of the peace, as I was blocking their van from leaving the site. The guys in the van were also drinking cans of beer while they were driving. About ten minutes later, a police dog unit arrived. I told the officer that the bikes were in the back of the travellers van, as I saw them being placed there when I arrived. The officer said he did not want to get them agitated as he had no back-up and would go and question them. They said they knew nothing about the bikes. The officer then asked me to move out of their way and let them go. He refused to search the van. Instead, he said he would talk to the other people in the caravans at the end of the lane. I could see he was trembling. I got out of my car with a metal bar, grabbed one traveller and dragged him from the van, and told them, I'm the fucking nasty off-duty police officer, and to open the back doors or I would put this over both their heads and have them locked up. They quickly opened the doors and pulled out the bikes. I called the officer back and told him I wanted them both charged with theft and drinking alcohol while driving on a public road. He said that I was to put the bar away and take the bikes and leave, or he would charge me with an offensive weapon and instigating a breach of the peace. I told him this is theft. He said he had spoken to the family, and they said to him that their five-year-old gypsy kid had got bolt cutters and had cut the chains, and he took the bikes, and the guys in the van did not know the kid had put the bikes in their van.

I told the officer that they were talking bollocks, and I explained that a five-year-old did not have the strength to use the bolt cutters cutting the chains and that most adults would struggle. The bike chains, bolt cutters, and angle grinders were in the back of their van when I took out the bikes. He said he was not taking this any further, as I had got the bikes back, and he didn't want any trouble kicking off while on his own there; I could see he was scared. I told him I was here for backing him up and stop being a pathetic coward in uniform. I told him I would be making an official complaint. I also stated that if it weren't for my threats to the guys that robbed the bikes and me blocking the exit, he would have let them drive away and got away with it. Again, he stated that he would not take this any further, and I should leave right now, or he would arrest me and take me down to the station. I told him that there was no way he would arrest me without backup.

He just turned and got in his police dog van and drove away. The two travellers in the van carried on drinking and drove off behind him. As I drove a few hundred yards down the road, two police cars were parked in the BP petrol station. I went walked in, and six coppers were chatting, eating, and drinking coffee at the tables. I asked why no one had come to assist with the traveller trouble up the road when their college called for help? They told me they were on their coffee break.

I said to them that the police are paid by our council tax contributions to enforce the law, not to be sitting here drinking coffee and saying amongst themselves, 'we're not going to help with any backup, as its travellers and we don't want to get hurt, so we won't answer our radios, and hope it will go away.' I have seen this happen with the police so many times before. (The BP petrol station gives free coffee and food to all uniformed officers).

I made an official complaint to the police chief and got a section written about it in the local papers. Still, nothing happened—just the usual bullshit standard police letter of how busy their officers are, with no apology about their officers. No wonder people have lost faith in our police. It is a known fact that the British police are terrified of arresting travellers; sadly, that's why they can commit many robberies, as they very rarely get investigated for crimes committed.

Similarly, our local post office got robbed very early one morning before Christmas by armed robbers who held the morning staff captive. They got away with a large amount of cash, cards, stamps, etc. There were CCTV cameras around the post office and in the lamp posts outside, as they have cameras on nearly every street in Luton. A few weeks later, I asked the manager at the post office if they caught the robbers. He said he had got a letter from the police just after the robbery, saying that they had no leads and it was not in their interest to continue this any further. They were dropping the case, and as the post office was covered by insurance, he would get the insurance money back. In other words, crime pays. They got away with it.

I had many friends in the police, and I drank with them at their private bar at Luton police station, where alcoholic drinks were half the price as local pubs. I could tell you some stories that would make you seethe with rage, with things they have got away with! But for now, that will remain confidential unless I write a different book on corrupt cops.

(Second rant over)

Facts (In the USA)

Ninety percent of bail jumpers are brought in to the authorities by bounty hunters. Law-enforcement officers arrest around five percent. Five percent remain at large.

In 1997, for instance, 33,000 defendants were given bail then skipped their court dates. Most were on drug-related or violent crime offences or theft.

Bounty hunters started to wear police-like uniforms because the police frequently mistook them for criminals. When you are chasing a dangerous criminal with a gun in your hand, the police may arrive and take you for a criminal with a gun and shoot you instead.

We often wear police-like uniforms and use police and SWAT[23] equipment, all in black with Polartec masks, etc. We carry two handguns, shotguns, machine guns, mace and pepper spray, handcuffs, batons. We also wear bulletproof caps and vests. We also have X26 Tasers and stun grenades because you need to intimidate fugitives. Most fugitives are extremely violent, unpredictable, and won't return to jail peacefully, especially when they know they will face a long haul in prison.

It has now become law that bounty hunters should wear clothing with 'Bail Recovery Agents' on their uniforms' front and back. You have to be licensed and bonded in a few states, but most states don't require a licence or gun permit.

---

[23] See glossary

A lot of bounty hunters brag about being highly trained and experienced in all manners of martial arts. I met one young bounty hunter in the States, who told me he was a sixth Dan karate black belt. He was only twenty-five years old. I know from experience it takes three to five years to reach the first black belt, two more years to get the second Dan, three more years to get third, etc. I asked him if he wrote out his own grades on paper, as he must have started training when he was six months old. I showed him my licence and asked to see his—he refused to show me his licence!

When I worked with a bounty hunters team later on in my career, we all carried the same Sig Sauer 9mm 226 semi-auto pistols. Why? —because it matched our uniforms! No, rubbish! It's because, if you got into a shoot-out, you could share ammo clips, as all guns we used are the same model.

We use many people to obtain information, including paid snitches, the police, DEA, and FBI agents.

People used to think I was over-cautious because I always wore my bulletproof vest and packed a gun with me everywhere I went, to restaurants, coffee bars, even to the grocery store.

But after you have seen and done some of the things I have, you never know, one night you may be going out for an innocent drink, and a psychopath comes along and decides to blow your brains out. He may even recognise me as someone who put his brother or family member away for a long time.

I remember once having to go into a redneck bar in Beattyville, Appalachia. To arrest one of their kind, the guy I was trying to capture was a stocky hillbilly that threatened me, and he quickly pulled out a large bowie knife from his waistband and held it to my throat. I had my hands up while he carried on drinking his full glass of beer. I saw a chance and punched the bottom of the glass into his face and then pulled out my gun and cracked him at the side of his face, knocking him out on the bar floor, pity the bar had a few people drinking in there, as I would have put a few shots into him as he lay there bleeding on the floor. When I had the situation under control, I then called for the paramedics and police.

Shooting Practice

I remember when a film company flew over from London to film a documentary about my USA work. I had taken them out to a day's shooting practice at our 100-acre shooting ground, which was a beautiful scenic site with Mount Rainier in the background. I had placed some bowling skittles down the range and stuck Swan Vesta 'strike anywhere' matches in the tops of the skittles.

These are the red ones you can light on virtually anything. I then drew my pistol and skimmed the bullets across the matches' tops without breaking them, causing the match to ignite. The film director decided not to show this clip to the public, as they thought the British police and security services might put me on their watch list when I returned to the UK.

One other time, I took another film crew out to our shooting range, but into the deep forest side, as they wanted to film us do our shooting practice. On the way there, it started pouring down with rain—and I don't mean average rain but severe torrential rain and strong wind. They thought we had better call it a day, but I told them no way! We will still shoot in this weather because when we are arresting skips, we have to learn to shoot accurately in all weather types and not call off an arrest because of pouring rain.

It looked great with the rain pouring down and soaking us to the skin, water flowing from our cap peaks, and our guns steaming. Later, when the rain slowed down, I let the film crew have a shoot. I still have the photos. They used the pistols with one hand and held umbrellas with the other hand, typical English.

What a sight it was to see!

When we were out filming again at our private range near Mount Rainier in Washington, we decided to try a couple of things we had seen in movies. What would happen if you shot a full propane cylinder and petrol tank on a car? Would they explode like they do in the movies?

Remember, bullets are made of brass and lead. Unless you are shooting FMJ (Full Metal Jacket)—then it might be possible for an FMJ round to ricochet off a metal surface and cause a spark, but a lead bullet will not spark. Even if an FMJ did spark on metal from a ricochet near fuel, the fuel would need the correct mix of 90% oxygen, 10% petrol vapour to ignite.

We got four old bangers (cars) from the scrap yard and took them to our shooting ground. We also took a few full cylinders of propane gas, some small and some large cylinders. We set them all up on the range, with the two cars half full of fuel/petrol, and the gas canisters were also full. We set up a protection screen at a safe distance to get behind in case they did explode, and we also filled up two one-gallon, see-through plastic milk containers with petrol and put them down the range.

I fired 9mm rounds into the propane gas canisters at twenty-five yards, and all they did was dent the canisters. I fired six 9mm shots into one car's fuel tank, and all it did was piss out fuel from the bullet holes. We then fired an AR-15 machine gun, emptying the full clip into the fuel tank—same thing, lots of holes pissing out fuel. Then we fired FMJ's into the propane gas canisters, and they just blew out a gas cloud at pressure from the bullets going straight through, but nothing exploded. We shot at the plastic milk cartons filled with the petrol; same thing, no explosion. So the Hollywood films do look like they are just a myth—but what did work, If there was a flame alight near the gas canister or petrol tank when the bullet hit the tank. The flame ignited the fuel, and it did explode, the same with the gas cylinders. A friend from the army told me later that if you shot a mini Gatling gun using FMJs at a gas cylinder, it would explode as he tried it, and it worked. I have never tried this, so if you fired bullets, FMJ, or even Tracer rounds (these glow with flames when shot) at a car fuel tank, it would not explode unless you are in the movies, of course.

Another exploding target we regularly used was Tannerite. It is a brand of binary explosive used for firearms practice. And it is sold as two separate components. It can be transported and sold in many states without any legal restrictions that would otherwise apply to explosives.

The best thing about using Tannerite targets is a massive explosion when it is shot with a high-velocity bullet. But if you hit it with a low-velocity bullet or shotgun round, there was a good chance it may not explode straight away.

The reaction occurs at a very high velocity, producing a large vapour cloud and a loud report; it is marketed as 'useful for long-range target practice': the shooter does not need to walk downrange to see if the target has been hit. The target will react and serve as an obvious indicator.

Binary explosives like Tannerite are also used in licensed business applications, including commercial blasting, product testing, and special effects. Everything is available in the States to have a fantastic shooting time, including hunting.

MISCELLANEOUS INFORMATION

Equipment that I used and carried:
Plus, some of the items I always carried in my truck and why.

Bounty hunters, or bail enforcement agents, earn a living tracking, capturing, and delivering fugitives to jails, the police, and other authorities. Bounty hunters walk a fine line when it comes to their legal authority, as they can legally perform tasks usually reserved for police officers in specific situations. Unlike police officers, bounty hunters do not face criminals in large groups with armed backup and dispatcher co-ordination. Bounty hunters have to be fully equipped and prepared to take down some of the nation's most dangerous and desperate criminals, most of the time single-handedly.

The first thing you need is a reliable 4x4 truck with removable magnetic signs and equipped with leg chains. You will need a grill fixed inside between the front and back seats to stop skips attacking you while transporting them to the jail.

When you have found the skip, which is only the first step, actually getting him from his hiding place to jail can be the biggest challenge.

Some fugitives travel long distances to escape the law, possibly crossing multiple state lines even before an arrest warrant is issued. Long-distance travel is a large part of the bounty hunters' job, and all bounty hunters need vehicles that can thrive in virtually any condition.

Television reality star Dog the bounty hunter casts an

impressive shadow on his chopper motorcycle or standard van. Still, vehicles like these can become useless in a blizzard or rainstorm, on steep mountain gradients, or in an off-road pursuit. A four-wheel drive, off-road-capable vehicle with a reputation for long life and reliability is the best option for a professional bounty hunter. Still, they cost big bucks, and most novice bounty hunters cannot afford this luxury.

***

Dwayne Chapman:
The first time I met Dog and Beth were when we were doing the *Bounty Hunter* TV series. In walked this scruffy loudmouthed biker, shouting at the top of his voice, and with him, his big-chested blonde wife both were dressed like scruffy bikers—I thought they were the skips being brought in, not the bounty hunters.

In his TV series, he wears:
Open shirts and medallions are hanging/long wrestler-type hair. (Will get grabbed while making an arrest).
Designer gear clothes are not practical for making arrests.
Earrings will get ripped out.
Pointed-toe shoes with metal toe caps.
No guns, only pepper-ball guns—no use against real guns!
And Dog says prayers with his skips before locking them up; this was all posing for the show, as you can't run and chase after a fleeing skip in all this gear.

What equipment you actually need in this job:
A bullet-proof and stab-proof vest, for wearing on top or underneath a shirt, a Kevlar ball cap, and a helmet.

Uniform with 'Recover Agent' on display.

Plenty of guns.

Mace and pepper spray.

Steel toecap boots for kicking in doors.

It would help if you always had a 'USA/POLICE' working area book with you for every state you work in.

Reverse directories: these are phone books that list the telephone numbers and gives you the address they are registered to.

Crossbow. Many uses, including hunting.

Compound bow and arrows. Many uses, including hunting.

Silencers for pistol and rifle and lots of ammunition.

Camouflage and Ghillie suit, black balaclava.

Camouflage black face paint (day and night use).

Night vision goggles/car trackers.

38mm snub nose pistol for my ankle holster and used as a back-up pistol.

Sniper rifle. Submachine gun. Pump-action, or SPAS-12 shotgun.

M84 stun grenades (flashbangs).

A one-person tent, sleeping bag, two-way radio, two cell phones, and spare batteries.

Complete first aid kit.

Canon EOS camera and telescopic lens.

It would help if you had an Air rifle, bag of marbles, catapult, and a reverse peephole viewer.

The reverse peephole viewer was a small device that I put on the outside door viewer, enabling me to see the entire inside of the room.

The air rifle and catapult I used to shoot out street lights while I was on night surveillance. This makes less noise than a gun, and it's a lot cheaper. Sometimes I used the catapult to fire a marble or stones at a skip's door, so I could see who looked out or opened it.

Compass, maps, binoculars, etc.

Taser, stun guns, mace or pepper spray, gas masks, and eye-protection goggles.

Four sets of handcuffs, nylon ties, hogties, ankle chains, body strap, to lock their hands in cuffs on a body belt around them onto their body, and a pair of extra-large handcuffs for big guys' wrists.

Spit hood or duct tape for defendants' mouths, if they spit or give verbal abuse, plus many other uses.

Identification and a badge were hanging around your neck.

A survival knife with a saw-edge blade plus a sewing kit for repairs, any injuries or cuts requiring stitching, especially when a hospital is not around, these items are fitted into the knife's handle.

A winch, this was in case my truck got stuck in the mud, etc. I could then use the winch to pull it out using a tree trunk. I also used the winch to pull out iron security grills on house doors before smashing them down.

Complete lock-picking kit.

Door entry equipment/ rams/levers/crowbars etc.

MRE ration kits (Meal Ready to Eat). You can eat them for up to twenty-one days, and they have a shelf life of three years, coffee, water, etc.

Food for horse and pony. Because of the vast forests, woodlands, and mountainous terrain in the USA, you can't always use a truck, so sometimes you use a horse.

And of course, throw-down guns:

Throw-downs guns are illegal guns; you take off criminals when you arrest them and don't hand them in, and you keep them, just in case you shoot an unarmed person. Then you will need to put their fingerprints onto the guns and bullets. It's not enough just to place the weapon in their hand or nearby, to stand up in courts in the USA. And yes! Illegal to do. I have so many true stories to tell. About how many times I got arrested and thrown in jail in the States, and never having any charges stick against me. I often had to use throw-down weapons because the skip didn't have a gun when I shot him. I never knew what they were until the police and FBI told me how to use them.

Once a sheriff in a small town in Texas stated when I was tracking a skip for murder hiding in his town. "When you find this nigger, shoot him in the head and put a throw-down weapon in his hand if he has no gun when killing him! We won't be asking you any questions, nor will there be any charges to face in a court of law!"

Modern Times:

Nowadays, bounty hunters have got it so easy; with cameras, Sat-Nav's, iPhones, computer equipment, roaming Internet, and body cameras, they can save a lot of time and money tracking down fugitives while using the Internet and satellite navigation.

Alias Names, Street Names, and False Passports:

The Yanks used to call me 'Seagull' or that's what I thought they we calling me. Later, when I asked why Seagull, they told me when I arrested people, I looked and acted like Steven Seagal—plus, I had a ponytail like him. I had never heard of Seagal, and they told me to watch the film *Hard to Kill*.

I should mention that when I was operating in the States, I was using many alias names, with fake passports, ID cards, business cards, etc. This was for my own safety because the last thing you need is some smart-ass gang-banger or drug dealer finding out who you are and where you live and carrying out his threats to kill you.

Here are just a few of my 'Alias-Names' and a few 'Street-Names' I used:

Buddy Love, Grizzly bear
Cruz Cabrette, Sharkee
Danny Platt, Black Raven
Nick Ramayo, Trigger Hap
John De-silva, X-Term
Kip Taylor, Rumbo-Gumbo
Snype and Eugene McGraw.

Passports:

I had many passports under different names; sometimes, I even forgot what my real name was! In those days, they were easy to obtain if you knew where to get a false passport.

I regularly travelled on them out of the country and in and out of the UK without any problems. I remember once I had a slight problem with one passport. I got into some aggravation in Dunstable, Bedfordshire. The detective, who said he knew me, was questioning where my real passport was, as he knew that could not be the real name I was using. I travelled back and forth to the States on a different passport without any problems. One passport I had was obtained by a close friend in the FBI. This one was always the best one to use for overseas travel, as it was authentic.

Examples of Misdemeanours versus Felonies:

A crime can have the same general classification and can also be broken down into several different severity levels, some of which may raise the seriousness from a misdemeanor to a felony. These are examples:

Assault:

An excellent example of multiple levels of severity is the general class of crime referred to as assault. In the case of assault, threatening to cause harm a person but not carrying through on the threat would be classified as a misdemeanor. An assault that resulted in actual bodily injury or a weapon used as part of the assault would be considered a felony.

Theft:

Theft is another example of a crime that has different levels of severity. Petty theft is the unlawful taking of property or money from another person without their consent. The distinction between whether theft is a misdemeanor or a felony is dependent on the value of the cash or property stolen. Many states consider theft of up to $500 a misdemeanor and larger amounts to be a felony. A felony theft can be referred to as larceny.

Indecent Exposure:

These crimes are also distinguished as misdemeanors or felonies, depending on whom the crime was committed against. These crimes fall into the following category: Exposing one's private parts in public in such way as to alarm others is considered to be a misdemeanor. However, if the exposure is before a child, then the crime rises to the level of a felony.

Different states set different age limits to where the line exists between a misdemeanor and felony indecent exposure.

Traffic Violations:

In most instances, traffic violations are classified as a misdemeanor. Here are some examples of traffic misdemeanor violations, which include:

Speeding.

Driving without a licence (DWL).

Driving without insurance (DWI).

Driving under the influence (DUI).

Felony traffic violations include: leaving the scene of an accident and vehicular homicide.

Another potential felony traffic infraction is a person having repeated DUIs. In this case, many states upgrade repeated charges of DUI from misdemeanor to felony status. While the criminal act is committed, it is the same. Multiple violations can result in a felony charge that carries harsher punishments.

Jail Time for Misdemeanours versus Felonies:

The primary difference between misdemeanors and felonies is the amount of jail time that a convicted offender can be sentenced to serve. Many felonies are broken down into different classifications or seriousness levels according to what punishments may be imposed.

Felonies are broken down into these different classifications and include:

Murder.

Rape.

Arson.

Sale of illegal drugs.

Grand theft.

Kidnapping.

These felonies can be classified from Class E or F felonies, such as the lowest theft levels, up to Class A felonies, which carry a life's sentence in prison or even the death penalty. Class A felonies are generally for murder or a first-degree intentional homicide.

Severity of Punishments:

The classification of misdemeanors and felonies is legally based on the severity of punishments, and the most severe penalties are reserved for the most severe offenses. Traffic violations, trespass, petty theft, and similar crimes are misdemeanors and, depending on the state, carry maximum jail times of between six months and one year. The attendant fines are also limited to relatively small amounts of money, generally $1,000 to $2,000 maximum.

Felonies such as murder, rape, arson, and kidnapping are substantially more severe. They all carry jail times of at least one year and substantially greater incarceration terms in most cases. At the most stringent level of felony classification, Class A, the maximum penalty can be life imprisonment without parole or the death penalty.

***

Survival courses:

Throughout the mid-1970s, I was still going on police combat shoots at The Bisley shooting camp and the clay shoots at Broomhills gun club in Markyate, Luton. I was also a regular pigeon shooter with a pump-action shotgun in the local woods in Caddington, Bedfordshire. I had not planned to go on any survival courses; I was also running a paintball team in my local bar/restaurant, The Casa Bianca, in Luton town centre, owned by an Italian friend of mine called Tony. We were called The Casa Bianca Paintball Team. I had got together a team for the Sunday event Woburn Woods, and an ex-army friend of mine wanted to join in, called Pete. In those days, the paintballs were still biodegradable but were not very waterproof, and if it rained, which it often did when we played, your paintballs got wet and melted in your gun, causing continual jam-ups.

While we were out playing pretend war, Pete and I were crawling through the brush; he started to tell me about a survival course he was going on in a few weeks. I was intrigued! When we got back to base, I asked him more about this survival course and could I book it and bring my M16 semi-automatic rifle with me, as it was licensed? He explained that the course was an introductory wilderness survival course; one took place on the Brecon Beacons in South Wales. Most of the people on it were ex-army, and not many civilians attended these courses; it was going to be a two-week course that would cost about £1,000 in those days.

We were informed that a helicopter would drop us at a specific location, we were to bring with us a backpack, sleeping bag, knife, canteen, a tin mug and a good pair of walking boots, a good hat, gloves, etc., The instructors would show us how to make hunting weapons, like a bow, arrows, spears, axes, and we would have to hunt animals for food. So I signed the waiver, paid the fee, and went.

It was fascinating to ride in a helicopter for the first time. After a brief training talk with nine guys, most were ex-army, everybody was dressed in BDUs[24], our two instructors talked like they may have been ex SAS, which added more excitement to the trip. It was like I was going into a war zone.

We landed on a hillside in the pouring rain, and we were all given a primary two days' ration of dry snacks and water. After that, we had to survive on what we hunted or found. Our instructors had two-way radios to call in for help if someone got severely injured or sick or could not hack it! And they would fail and would be taken out, no refunds! Some of us had brought some gear to the course like sandwiches, flasks of coffee, choc bars, and telephones were confiscated. Then we all watched the helicopters take off and disappear from view—and then silence, except for the rain!

I was excited and terrified all at once. I did not want to fail this course and request to leave because I could not hack it! Especially as our instructors informed us that we were going to be walking up and down mountings, crossing rivers, foraging for plants and grubs to eat, eating bugs, hunting animals, taught how to drink our piss, and learning how to navigate in the dark with a compass and the stars. We were a team and had to pull together, and as the instructors told us or shouted orders at us. "Only fucking weak pussies get left behind!" and, "If you leave, you will always be branded as a fucking weak pussy!" Actually, the instructors were scarier than what lay ahead of us all for two weeks. After six gruelling days, I will admit I struggled with the course; two guys had already pulled out—couldn't hack it!

"Go fucking pussies!" they got us all to chant!

"Pussies, weak pussies!" was the last thing they heard as they were airlifted out and told by our instructors that they were a fucking disgrace to the team. I carried on. I did not want to be humiliated and branded a fucking pussy.

One morning we were woken early and told us to bring our tin mugs with us. We collected worms in the dew at the crack of dawn; we got loads, so we all went back to camp, excited that we were going to go fishing for breakfast. We were starving. Even though I had not seen a river nearby, I was excited it was fish for breakfast. We made a fire, and yes, you guessed it—the worms were our breakfast. The instructors told us not to think worms but chicken, or we would bring them up, get sick, and become pussies. If we didn't eat what we were told to, we would lack the nourishment to go on the next day's gruelling trek, as we had a time frame to get to the base to be airlifted back to normality, with the promise of a cold beer and real-food.

For the time being, we had to do with worms and distilled piss for breakfast. Everything that moved: bugs, rats, birds were 'chicken,' and when you are starving, it tasted delicious, just like real chicken. Later we were taught how to catch dew or moisture for drinking water. For example, you made a hole, placed a can on the centre of a poly sheet made into a cone shape. The sun's heat raises the air and soil temperature below, and vapour is produced on the poly sheet and runs into the cup. They also showed us how to get water from plants, and later we went fishing when we found water.

After two hard, gruelling weeks, base camp was in sight. Only six of us left; our two instructors, me, Pete, and two others. It was odd how you saw the end of the course in the distance. Even though it was five miles walk away, and you somehow got a surge of strength to carry on like an injection of energy into your tired and weak body.

We had made it. I had lost a lot of weight, but I felt good. We all went to the local pub and had a nice cold beer; it tasted so good, but not as good as the instructors' praise for finishing the course. The Instructors told us that we could eat anything, but not to gulp it down, as our bodies would not cope and we would be sick or ill—but fucking hell, I felt so much pain in my life now that the course was over! After a few days, everything started to go back to normality, but I was so proud I had finished the course. I said I would never do another one ever again, but that was a lie as I did three more courses while working in the States. —I needed to learn how to survive alone while tracking people down in the States' vast terrain.

Survival USA

The States' survival courses were very similar in a way, but because of bears, wolves, snakes, and dangerous wild animals, we were allowed to take guns, a rifle, and a pistol; this was when I was first introduced to MREs. (Meals Ready to Eat)

On the States' survival courses, you get wilderness, urban, and arctic, extreme weather conditions. With urban survival, they teach you how to cope in real situations if there was a natural disaster; no electricity, water, gas, similar to in a wilderness: how to light fires and cook, keep warm, disposing of human waste and contamination—like a zombie apocalypse. Much more to fit real-life situations and did benefit me with the tracking jobs I was about to take on.

I did very few survival courses in the UK; they were mostly in the States. The only reason was that I was tracking a lot of people out in the wilderness. I had to make sure I knew how to survive independently because if you do get into difficulty in the wilderness, you cannot ring for help as there will be no cell phone signal. You will be on your own if you get injured; you need to know how to hunt wild animals and what to do if animals attacked you—I always had bear repellent with me.

Unless you have been to the States and seen how vast the forests and terrains are, you just cannot imagine how dangerous it can be in these dense forest areas and mountains. The Olympic Peninsula rain forest and mountains are 5,000 square miles of mountains and thick forest. It's easy to murder and bury the body out there, never to be found. More murders go unsolved in these areas. People just disappear, never to be seen again in these dense forest areas.

These are a few of the things taught in the courses:
All equipment was supplied on the courses, except guns, but you still had to do gun safety before starting.

Understanding how to keep warm or cool.

How to make shelters.

Lighting fires with flint and steel.

How to light a fire and make utensils to cook.

How to make water safe.

Dangers of wild water, medical aspects, dehydration, heat exhaustion, and malnutrition, etc.

How to find food in the wild, hunt, and make weapons from the surrounding wilderness.

How to forage and find food from plants, roots, and seeds.

Dangerous plants and toxins.

Medical issues, how to sew up large wounds and gashes with needle and thread.

How to make signals, mirrors, flashlights, etc.

Astronavigation and map sketching.

Tracking animal and human footprints.

How to make snares and traps.

Nature awareness, which could save your life.

Hunting and how to skin animals for food and use fur for clothing etc.

And much, much more. Too much to list.

Hopefully, later in these books, this will give you some idea of why I had to do these courses and how they helped my survival when tracking people.

Reality television:

In the Bear Grylls TV series, he says, "The contestants must fight their for survival." I knew it was impossible to take a group of twenty-eight people into the wild and just leave them there, to survive on their own for six weeks without any survival training! How the hell is someone with no training going to find safe water to drink—and how are they going to hunt wild animals? It's not that easy and even harder when you are hungry and thirsty!

I knew American wrestling was fake, and so was *The only way is Essex,* the reality TV show; again, they all have a script. It didn't surprise me when I read that the Bear Grylls survival shows were also partly faked, as the show producers will make sure water and food are left around. Animals are released nearby to make it easier to catch and eat, as they have a duty of care to the contestants. Bullshit! That's not real survival skills; it's like a picnic in the woods.

When we filmed our reality bounty hunter series in the States, nothing was faked or manufactured. They filmed it as it happened. Nothing was cut out from the show, and even the mistakes we made were aired, including raiding the wrong address, getting hurt, or punched in the face. Even the American reality show *Cops* made mistakes, and that got shown.

When I did the *Bounty Hunter* series after meeting with Samantha Dolenz, Mickey Dolenz's wife from the sixties pop group the Monkey's, I was informed the cameraman and sound man would be with us every day and night to film it as it happened. The only thing they would not film was too much violence, i.e., shootings, kills, macho shots, or faked arrests. We would only get paid for an authentic real-life arrest. They did not want to show the violent side, as bounty hunters had already got a bad name at the time, as there had been several shoots to kill regularly happening, some skips were unarmed and shot in the back by bounty hunters.

For me, it was a bonus—getting paid to find the skip and getting paid $500 a day for filming. Most of the time, I just got on with what I had to do and forgot the camera team was there. The worst bit about the Bounty Hunter series was that after you arrested the skips, you had to interview them on the way back to jail. Any violent incidents on the way to jail were cut, and it looked like the bounty hunters were nice and friendly people, the way we smiled and chatted to the prisoners like we were the most caring guys around. That part was a bit unrealistic. But the money was good, so who gives a shit how we are portrayed on television? I think we filmed over sixty episodes and I only saw about eight episodes on TV. Sadly, I only managed to record about six or seven of the shows, as I was always busy and had to ask friends to record the series for me if they had time. I will show a lot of these recordings on my web page after all the books are published.

***

Bail bonds and how it works:

The more serious the crime, the higher the bail amount is set. Sometimes for the most dangerous criminals, bail is set very high, or no bail at all—they must remain in police custody. Not everyone accused of a crime can afford bail money, which can run into the hundreds of thousands, if not millions of dollars. In those cases, a bail bond agent will step in and put up a bail bond—sort of like a loan—in return for a percentage, usually ten percent of the total bail.

For this reason, the bondsmen usually require collateral from the accused, such as property, a car, or boat title. As bail bond companies are liable for the full bail bond amount if they fail to appear on their court date, the police can't always look for defendants that skipped bail, so many bondsmen hire a professional bounty hunter to track down the skips for them.

More than one bounty hunter may be assigned to the same case, but professional bail recovery agents tend to shy away from cases with too much competition. In return for their services, bounty hunters receive ten percent of the total bail bond, plus costs. An experienced bounty hunter who works eighty to one hundred and fifty cases can earn anywhere from $100,000 to $200,000 annually. But the hours are long and gruelling, sometimes eighty to a hundred hours a week, and the work is challenging. I once said, "As bounty hunters, we're driving around bad neighbourhoods, talking to stupid people, drinking cold coffee, and looking for violent bad guys—and they talk about the glory of it all!"

Bounty hunters are much more effective than the police. According to some of the Bail Bond Associations, they nab nearly ninety percent of all bail jumpers.

Laws in the US

In the United States' legal system, the 1872 US Supreme Court case Taylor versus Taintor, 16 Wall (83 U.S. 366, 21 L. Ed. 287), was cited as having established that the person into whose custody an accused is remanded, as part of the accused bail, has sweeping rights to recover that person. However accurate this may have been when the decision was reached, the portion cited was obiter dicta[25] and had no binding precedential value.

A bail bondsman employs most bounty hunters: the bounty hunter is paid part of the bail the fugitive initially paid. If the fugitive eludes bail, the bondsman, not the bounty hunter, is responsible for the remainder of the fugitive's bail. Thus, the bounty hunter is the bail bondsman's way of ensuring his clients arrive at their trial. In the United States, bounty hunters catch an estimated 31,500 bail jumpers per year; that's about 90% of people who jump bail. Bounty hunters are also sometimes known as 'fugitive recovery agents,' which are the preferred industry and polite terms, but they are still called 'bounty hunters' in everyday speech.

Bounty hunters are sometimes called 'skip tracers,' but this usage can be misleading. While bounty hunters are often called skip tracers, skip tracing is generally referred to as searching for an individual through less direct methods than active pursuit and apprehension, such as private investigators or debt collectors.

---

[25] See Glossary

Skip tracing can also refer to searches related to a civil matter and does not always imply criminal conduct on the part of the individual that is being traced.

In the United States of America, bounty hunters have varying authority levels in their duties concerning their targets, depending on the states in which they operate. As opined in the Taylor versus Taintor court case, and barring restrictions are applicable State by State, a bounty hunter can enter the fugitive's private property without a warrant to execute a re-arrest. In some states, bounty hunters do not undergo any formal training and are generally unlicensed, only requiring sanction from a bail bondsman to operate. In other States, however, they are now held to varying standards of training and licensure.

In California, bounty hunters must undergo a background check and complete various courses satisfying the penal code 1299 requirements. In some parts of the States, they are prohibited from carrying firearms without proper permits. Most states now require bounty hunters to wear clothing identifying them as such.

In Kentucky, bounty hunting is generally not allowed because the state does not have a bail bondsmen system and releases bailed suspects through the state's Pre-trial Services Division of the courts. Thus there is no bondsman with the right to apprehend the fugitive. Generally, only fugitives who have fled bail on federal charges from another state where bounty hunting is legal are allowed to be hunted in Kentucky. At the same time, every bounty hunter must be a peace officer, a Level III armed security officer, or a private investigator in the state of Texas. State legal requirements are often imposed on out-of-state bounty hunters, meaning a suspect could temporarily escape re-arrest by entering a state where the bail agent has limited or no jurisdiction.

International Laws and Legal Protection:
Bounty hunters can run into serious legal problems if they try to get fugitives from other countries. Laws in nearly all countries outside the US, which do not permit bounty hunters to operate, would label the re-arrest of any fugitive 'kidnapping' or the bail agent may incur the punishments of some other serious crime.

Noted bounty hunter Duane 'Dog' Chapman, the star of the TV series *Dog the Bounty Hunter,* was arrested in Mexico after apprehending the multi-millionaire rapist and fugitive, Andrew Luster. Chapman was later declared a fugitive by a Mexican prosecutor. He was subsequently arrested in the United States to be extradited to Mexico even though, under Mexico's citizen arrest law, Chapman and his crew acted under the proper policy and broke no other Mexican laws. Bounty hunters Daniel Kear and Timm Johnsen pursued and apprehended Sidney Jaffe at his residence in Toronto, Canada, and brought him back to the states. Kear and Johnsen were later extradited to Canada and convicted of kidnapping.

While the United States government generally allows bounty hunters' activities in the United States, the government is not tolerant of these activities when they cause problems with other sovereign nations. Several bounty hunters have also been arrested for killing a fugitive or apprehending the wrong person, mistaking them for an offender. Unlike police officers, they have no legal protections against injuries to non-fugitives and few legal protections against damages to their targets.

In a Texas case, bounty hunters Richard James and his partner Pearson were arrested in 2001 for felony charges during an arrest. The fugitive and his family levied the charges. Still, they were later dismissed against the hunters after the fugitive's wife shot a deputy sheriff in another arrest attempt of the county sheriff's fugitive department. The hunters sued the fugitive and family, winning the civil suit for malicious prosecution with a judgment amount of 1.5 million dollars.

***

When I worked in Kansas, USA:

Kansas allows individuals to carry guns in public, either openly or concealed, with no gun permit, background check, or training. It also enables individuals to buy and sell guns without conducting a background check or keeping a sale record. Likewise, assault weapons and high capacity ammunition magazines are not regulated in Kansas, nor does it allow local governments to do so. No reporting of lost/stolen firearms is required.

Bounty hunter facts and Information:

So you have just finished watching a show on TV, or maybe one of the bounty hunter movies, and you've decided that you want to become a one. By all appearances, it is a fascinating and financially rewarding business, and sometimes it is exhilarating. But most of the time, it has to be one of the worst jobs there is— long hours of boring surveillance that they never show on TV, extremely slow and tedious, and a lot of the time, even no pay at the end of the day.

Remember, you don't get paid if you don't find the skip. There are genuine hurdles that you must overcome to become a recovery agent. When you actually make a recovery, you face one of the most dangerous situations in law enforcement. You never know what's waiting behind the next door.

The first thing you need to do is forget what you've seen on

TV because that's all make-believe! If you've always wanted to be a police officer or a modern-day Wyatt Earp, then find a police force or sheriff's department to join if you're going to be a show-off or tough guy, then there is no place for you in this business, except in a body bag.

Someone has probably told you there was tons of easy money being a bounty hunter. There is always a story about somebody finding a million-dollar skip and making a hundred or two hundred grand plus expenses. Not to be one to bust your bubble, but there are very few million-dollar bonds written nowadays and, when one is written, it has so much collateral security attached to it, the defendant can't afford to run. Still, some do, especially when they know they are guilty.

Most bail bonds written are going to be secured with some form of collateral or indemnity guarantee. Most of the skips that recovery agents look for are in the one thousand to fifty thousand range, and most bail agents only pay ten percent recovery fees and no expenses. That's the reason that almost any bail agent can probably name all the recovery agents in the whole country that are full-time recovery agents and are successful and the agents who have profitable sideline recovery businesses. More money is made teaching wannabe bounty hunters in schools. Some teachers have never done recoveries in their lives, and reading it from a textbook, and it's all talk.

Most bail bond companies do an outstanding job of making sure their defendant appears in court. If the defendant goes to court, there is no one to recover. Most of the time, a defendant misses court; it's some SNAFU[26], either with the court itself, the defendant's lawyer, or a simple mistake on the defendant's part.

---

[26] See glossary

The other truth is that when a defendant fails to appear, most bail bondsmen make their own recoveries to save money. They won't turn it over to a recovery agent until they know they can't find the defendant and the bonds about to be forfeited by the court.

OK! So you're still bound and determined to be a recovery agent. Well, you've got a long hard road ahead of you if you're not a retiring law-enforcement officer or federal agent. The reality is that the bail bond company will not hire you without experience, and you can't get experience if you can't work. The first thing you have to do is find an existing recovery agent that you can work for, probably without the benefit of getting paid, and get some experience. But wait; let's talk about what it takes to be a recovery agent.

Not that many bail bond companies hire felons as recovery agents anymore, but some still do; you are too much of a liability if something goes wrong. But then, if you are a felon and you own a bonding company, things may be different look at Dog' Chapman, an ex-drug dealer and offender. He gets a TV show behind him. If you look like a biker, a gang-banger, or maybe even Wyatt Earp with your Stetson hat and duster coat— you can go home too. No one will hire a poser—we don't need that image around us; we want professionals who can get the job done, not TV characters who screw up and wind up on the ten o'clock news.

Okay, I know a few guys out there who look like that. But the reality is that they are former law enforcement or ex-government agents that have been doing this for a long time and are very good at what they do. Sad, but true—they can get away with it, and we can't!

Nobody ever said life was fair.

Many states now a day require licensing, and they require

that you attend a state-specific school. You'll need to check your state's laws and make sure you do what is needed. There are states where you can't be a recovery agent, such as Arkansas, Florida, Texas, Washington, and the non-bail states of Illinois, Kentucky, Oregon, and Wisconsin. If you get caught there, you'll end up in jail for kidnapping. And then there are states like Arizona, Connecticut, Indiana, Mississippi, New Hampshire, Nevada, and a few more, where if you don't hold a licence from that state, you'll wind up in jail as well. No money in that! Of course, you also need to know about the *Uniform Extradition Act* and be sure you comply with it in each state.

Okay, now back to finding you someone to work with. The reality is you will probably have to work for very little or no money for a year or two. Once you've gotten some experience, don't start sending e-mails and wasting cash on bail agencies' letters. They just get filed or thrown in the trash. The only way you're going to get hired is through referrals. You'll probably have to do some more work for someone you don't know and not get paid. I now won't even talk to a recovery agent referred by another bail agent I don't know. The real truth of the matter is simple—if you don't know any bail agents when you start, you will never get started if you are still bound and determined to become a recovery agent—good luck! You're certainly going to need it.

Federal Bail Warrants:

Nearly all 'bounty hunters' only work on state or county bail bonds. I worked on Federal bail. These are the most severe and risky forms of bail bonds and the most dangerous, and very few people understand the difference between state or county bails bonds and federal bail bonds.

When a federal crime has been committed, it usually involves racketeering, national security crimes against federal officers, threats against prosecutors and judges, drug-related offences, civil rights crimes, and crimes committed using the US Postal Service. It also becomes a federal crime if a felon commits serious crimes in more than one state and if the FBI is involved and issue a federal warrant. Only then can I get involved, but only if they authorise me and give me the contract to make the arrest.

Federal crimes fall under the jurisdiction of the Department of Justice, the Drug Enforcement Agency (DEA), the Secret Service, or the United States Postal Service. They are all investigated by the FBI, then prosecuted by a federal prosecutor, and tried in court by a federal judge.

When I did Federal bail warrants, not only was I paid by bonding companies that wrote Federal bail bonds, but I was also paid by the FBI, DEA, and EPA (Environment Protection Agency), whose rewards can range from $1,000 to $1,000,000.

The title 18 USCs 3059 code offers rewards up to $25,000, just for information that leads to the arrest of defendants on a federal bail warrant. Some even have a 'dead or alive' clause, but many of my skips on federal bail warrants were also featured on the 'America's Most Wanted' television program.

When a Federal crime is involved, the bail is set very high by the court, as the defendant is a risk to the state. If the defendant is released for even a short time, he is a significant risk to the court case. For instance, he could commit further offences or intimidate the witnesses.

Usually, the amount to be taken by a Federal bail bond can be as high as 15% to 20% cash down and collateral. Some bail companies in the state do write federal bail bonds, and because it's a federal case, they want to see that the collateral covers almost the full bail amount. The judge during the arraignment hearing will determine the amount of the bail. In Federal cases, it's not uncommon to have bail set at very high amounts to make the release more difficult, but, in my experience, some defendants can afford and find the cash in full upfront and get released, even for murder. Then they intimidate the witnesses, who are too scared to give evidence in court; in some cases, witnesses just completely vanish.

If the defendant fails to make his court date/appearance, the judge will determine the forfeiture date, and if the defendant has not been brought into court by that date, the money, which could be as high as $1,000,000, has to be paid in full to the US government.

Information about US Marshalls:

The US Marshal's office was created by the Judiciary Act of 1789. The legislative history of PA 00-99 does not discuss the issue of state marshals carrying firearms. Like the police, DEA and FBI, marshals can carry guns, but, like bounty hunters, they still need a permit, and they must buy their own gun.

Federal Marshals:

They mostly enforce the federal courts' orders and provide protection and security for judges, attorneys, witnesses, and others attending trials and proceedings. They are also involved, to some extent, in many initiatives launched by other federal law-enforcement agencies. They apprehend federal fugitives and operate the witness security program, sometimes called witness protection. Federal marshals transport or accompany federal prisoners who are in transit. At times, the attorney general may issue orders that involve civil disturbances or terrorist activities that the US marshals must execute. Marshals may also execute seizure orders for a property that criminals have acquired through illegal activities.

Posse Comitatus:

From the Latin phrase *'force of the country.'*

Posse Comitatus members oppose the US federal government; they refuse to pay any taxes or register for any type of car or firearms licence. They believe that there is no legitimate form of government or higher authority than the local County Sheriff. And therefore, there is a saying: if the local sheriff refuses to carry out its citizens' will, he shall be removed by the posse to the most populated intersection of the street in the township, and at high noon he should be hung by the neck until dead, the body to remain there until sundown as an example to whom would have subverted the law. (Pity we don't have this law in the UK for all our treacherous MP's and PM.

I will only briefly go into this next section, as I regularly train with the Posse Comitatus on their shooting ground. I have a few friends who were active members of the posse and became close to them. Still, after I realised that I never saw any black members training on the land, I never joined their movement, and later I realised that they were affiliated with the Ku Klux Klan.

Many posse members practised survivalism and are involved in the American armed militia movement. When I was training with the posse, I was surprised to see how many vast acres of land and forests they owned. They had armed guards at each entrance. It was like you were on a fully equipped army base. With wooden huts, shops, and hospitals, they had plenty of everything from fully automatic machine guns, large ammunition stocks, many underground nuclear bunkers, tanks, (SAM's) surface to air missiles, rocket launchers, explosives, hundreds of boxes of hand grenades, etc. Very seldom do the feds or police try to enter their lands uninvited, as they know there will be a bloody shootout.

The Second Amendment to the United States Constitution: A well-regulated militia, being necessary to secure a free state, the people's right to keep and bear arms shall not be infringed.

APPENDIX

Decision of the 1872 United States Supreme Court Ruling Taylor versus Taintor, 156 Wall, 366.

This is the ruling all bail enforcement agents work under today:

When bail is given, the principal[27] is regarded as delivered to the sureties' custody (the bail bondsman). Their dominion[28] is a continuance of the original imprisonment. Whenever they choose to do so, they may seize and deliver him up in their discharge, and if that cannot be done at once, they may imprison him until it can be done. They may exercise their rights in person or by agent (a bounty hunter). They may pursue him into another state, may arrest him on the Sabbath, and, if necessary, may break and enter his house for that purpose.

The seizure is not made by virtue of a new process. None is needed. It is likened to the re-arrest by the sheriff of an escaping prisoner.

Hungerford Massacre:

The Hungerford massacre was a series of random shootings in Hungerford, England, on 19th August 1987, when Michael Ryan fatally shot sixteen people, including a police officer, before shooting himself. The Hungerford shootings at several different

---

[27] See glossary
[28] See glossary

locations, including a school Ryan, had once attended, using a handgun and two semi-automatic rifles. Ryan walked through the streets, shooting people at random. Fifteen other people were also shot but survived. There has never been a motive for the killings. However, one psychologist has theorised Ryan's justification for the massacre had been a form of 'anger and contempt for the ordinary life' around him, which he himself was not a substantial part of.

Home Secretary Douglas Hurd commissioned a report on the massacre. The Firearms (Amendment) Act 1988 was written into law in the wake of the incident, which bans the ownership of semi-automatic center-fire rifles and restricts the use of shotguns with a capacity of more than three cartridges.

Dunblane Massacre:

The second massacre was on 13th March 1996, a former scout leader Thomas Hamilton entered the gym at Dunblane primary school. He opened fire on a class of five and six-year-olds, killing sixteen children and their teacher before killing himself. In a shooting spree that lasted less than three minutes, Hamilton, armed with two pistols and two revolvers, fired a total of one hundred and nine rounds.

A public inquiry into the Dunblane massacre found that Hamilton was a former shopkeeper and had been previously investigated by the police, following complaints about his behaviour towards young boys. Hamilton was also once described by the police as dishonest, devious, and deceitful, yet! The police let him keep his firearms certificate and refused to disarm him. I see it as the police were partly to blame for this incident.

It remains the deadliest mass shooting in British history.

Habeas Corpus Act 1679:

This was an Act of the Parliament of England that was passed during King Charles II's reign to define and strengthen the ancient prerogative writ of habeas corpus, whereby persons unlawfully detained can be ordered to be prosecuted before a court of law.

Habeas Corpus is an Act of Parliament, still in force today, which ensures that no person can be imprisoned unlawfully. Translated, 'habeas corpus' means 'you may have the body' (if legal procedures are satisfied). This act may sound like a strange phrase, but it was the expression used to bring a prisoner into court in medieval times. It later became used to fight against arbitrary detention by the authorities.

The act laid out certain temporal and geographical conditions under which prisoners had to be brought before the courts. Jailors were forbidden to move prisoners from one prison to another or out of the country to evade the writ. In cases of disobedience, jailers would be punished with severe fines, which had to be paid to the prisoner.

Responding to abusive detention of persons without legal authority, public pressure on the English Parliament caused them to adopt this act. This established a critical right that was later written into the Constitution for the United States of America.

Habeas Corpus Act 1679

{A writ of habeas corpus: "may you have the body" is a writ or legal action that requires a person who has been arrested or imprisoned to be brought to a judge or into court}

It was an act to secure the subject's liberty better and prevent imprisonments beyond the seas.

I. Whereas great delays have been used by sheriffs, gaolers

(Jailers) and other officers, to whose custody, any of the King's subjects have been committed for criminal or supposed criminal matters, in making returns of writs of habeas corpus to them directed, by standing out an alias and pluries (many times) habeas corpus, and sometimes more, and by other shifts to avoid their yielding obedience to such writs, contrary to their duty and the known laws of the land, whereby many of the King's subjects have been, and hereafter may be long detained in prison, in such cases whereby law they are bailable, to their outstanding charges and vexation.

***

II. (1) For the prevention whereof, and the more speedy relief of all persons imprisoned for any such criminal or supposed criminal matters; (2) be it enacted by the King's most excellent Majesty, by and with the advice and consent of the lords spiritual and temporal, and commons, in this present Parliament assembled, and by the authority thereof. That when so ever any person or persons shall bring any habeas corpus directed unto any sheriff or sheriffs, gaoler, (Jailer) minister or other person whatsoever, for any person in his or their custody, and the said writ shall be served upon the said officer, or left at the gaol (Jail) or prison with any of the under-officers, under-keepers or deputy of the said officers or keepers, that the said officer or officers, his or their under-officers, under-keepers or deputies, shall within three days after the service thereof as aforesaid (unless the commitment aforesaid were for treason or felony, plainly and specially expressed in the warrant of commitment) upon payment or tender of the charges of bringing the said prisoner, to be ascertained by the judge or court that awarded the same, and endorsed upon the said writ, not exceeding twelve pence per mile, and upon security given by his own bond to pay the charges of carrying back the prisoner, if he shall be remanded by the court or judge to which he shall be brought according to the true intent of this present act, and that he will not make any escape by the way, make return of such writ; (3) and bring or cause to be brought the body of the party so committed or restrained, unto or before the lord chancellor, or lord keeper of the great seal of England for the time being, or the judges or barons of the said court from which the said writ shall issue, or unto and before such other person or persons before whom the said writ is made returnable, according to the command thereof; (4) and shall then likewise certify the true causes of his detainer or imprisonment, unless the commitment of the said party be in any place beyond the distance of twenty miles from the place or places where such court or person is or shall be residing; and if beyond the distance of twenty miles, and not above one hundred miles, then within the space of ten days, and if beyond the distance of one hundred miles, then within the space of twenty days, after such delivery aforesaid, and not longer.

***

III. (1) And to the intent that no sheriff, gaoler or other officer may pretend ignorance of the import of such writ; (2) be it enacted by the authority aforesaid, That all such writs shall be marked in this manner, Per statutum tricesimo primo Caroli secundi Regis, (During established thirty-second of King Charles) and shall be signed by the person that awards the same; (3) and if any person or persons shall be or stand committed or detained as aforesaid, for any crime, unless for felony or treason plainly expressed in the warrant of commitment, in the vacation-time, and out of term, it shall and may be lawful to and for the person or persons so committed or detained (other than persons convict or in execution of legal process) or any one on his or their behalf, to appeal or complain to the lord chancellor or lord keeper, or any one of his Majesty's justices, either of the one bench or of the other, or the barons of the exchequer of the degree of the coif; (4) and the said lord chancellor, lord keeper, justices or barons or any of them, upon view of the copy or copies of the warrant or warrants of commitment and detainer, or otherwise upon oath made that such copy or copies were denied to be given by such person or persons in whose custody the prisoner or prisoners is or are detained, are hereby authorized and required, upon request made in writing by such person or persons, or any on his, her, or their behalf, attested and subscribed by two witnesses who were present at the delivery of the same, to award and grant an habeas corpus under the seal of such court whereof he shall then be one of the judges; (5) to be directed to the officer or officers in whose custody the party so committed or detained shall be, returnable immediate before the said lord chancellor or lord keeper or such justice, baron or any other justice or baron of the degree of the coif of any of the said courts; (6) and upon service thereof as aforesaid, the officer or officers, his or their under-officer or under-officers, under-keeper or under-keepers, or their deputy in whose custody the party is so committed or detained, shall within the times respectively before limited, bring such prisoner or prisoners before the said lord chancellor or lord keeper, or such justices, barons or one of them, before whom the said writ is made returnable, and in case of his absence before any other of them, with the return of such writ, and the true causes of the commitment and detainer; (7) and thereupon within two days after the party shall be brought before them, the said lord chancellor or lord keeper, or such justice or baron before whom the prisoner shall be brought as aforesaid, shall discharge the said prisoner from his imprisonment, taking his or their recognizance, with one or more surety or sureties, in any sum according to their discretions, having regard to the quality of the prisoner and nature of the offense, for his or their appearance in the court of the King's bench the term following, or at the next assizes, sessions or general gaol-delivery of and for such county, city or place where the commitment was, or where the offense was committed, or in such other court where the said offense is properly cognizable, as the case shall require, and then shall certify the said writ with the return thereof, and the said recognizance or recognizance's unto the said court where such appearance is to be made; (8) unless it shall appear unto the said lord chancellor or lord keeper or justice or justices, or baron or barons, that the party so committed is detained upon a legal process, order or warrant, out of some court that hath jurisdiction of criminal matters, or by some warrant signed and sealed with the hand and seal of any of the said justices or barons, or some justice or justices of the peace, for such matters or offenses for the which by the law the prisoner is not bailable.

***

U.S. Code: Title 18:
CRIMES AND CRIMINAL PROCEDURE

Section: 3059. Rewards and appropriations, therefore:

(a)(1) There is authorized to be appropriated, out of any money in the Treasury not otherwise appropriated, the sum of $25,000 as a reward or rewards for the capture of anyone who is charged with violation of criminal laws of the United States or any State or of the District of Columbia, and an equal amount as a reward or rewards for information leading to the arrest of any such person, to be apportioned and expended in the discretion of, and upon such conditions as may be imposed by, the Attorney General of the United States. Not more than $25,000 shall be expended for information or capture of any one person.

(2) If any of the said persons shall be killed in resisting lawful arrest, the Attorney General may pay any part of the reward money at his discretion to the person or persons whom he shall adjudge to be entitled thereto. Still, no reward money shall be paid to any official or employee of the Department of Justice of the United States.

(b) The Attorney General each year may spend no more than $10,000 for services or information looking toward the apprehension of narcotic law violators who are fugitives from justice.

(c)(1) In exceptional circumstances and in the Attorney General's sole discretion, the information unknown to the Government relating to a possible prosecution under section 2326, which results in a conviction.

A person is not eligible for a payment under paragraph (Attorney General may make a payment of up to $10,000 to a person who furnishes)

(A) If the person is a current or former officer or employee of a Federal, State, or local government agency or instrumentality who furnishes information discovered or gathered in the course of Government employment;

(B) The person knowingly participated in the offense;

(C) The information furnished by the person consists of an allegation or transaction that has been disclosed to the public;

(i) In a criminal, civil, or administrative proceeding;

(ii) In a congressional, administrative, General Accounting Office report, hearing, audit, or investigation; or

(iii) by the news media, unless the person is the original source of information; or.

(D) When, in the Attorney General's judgment, it appears that a person whose illegal activities are being prosecuted or investigated could benefit from the award.

(3) For the purposes of paragraph (2)(C)(iii), the term "original source" means a person who has direct and independent knowledge of the information that is furnished and has voluntarily provided the information to the Government prior to disclosure by the news media.

(4) Neither the Attorney General's failure to authorize payment under paragraph (1) nor the amount authorized shall be subject to judicial review.

***

USA/Police Working Area Book:

When I was working between States in the USA, it was complicated to find the local police stations, prisons, contact lawyers, and prosecutors, especially when you have picked up a skip and found that the local police cells are full. Now you need to find out where to take them.

I was supplied an A4 size working area booklet covering each state I worked in. This booklet would give full information about where and whom to contact when I was in that state.

Here is the sort of information listed inside the booklet:

- A list of jail facilities in that state with the full address, telephone numbers, and cell times to accept prisoners.
- Telephone numbers for jail records and information.
- Security codes to get into the jail facilities' main booking desk and who to call to gain access codes.

- List of people and companies with private prison cells I could rent to put prisoners in if the police cells were full.
- List of all police, sheriff, and marshal's addresses and their contact numbers.
- List of bail bond companies and telephone numbers authorised to write bail bonds in that state.
- List of lawyers, prosecutors, and public defenders' offices in the area.
- Which police departments, and who to contact for auto and license plate records.
- FBI, DEA, ATF, and other department telephone numbers.
- Which codes to use for Justice, Superior, and Municipal courts.
- List of safe motels to stay in overnight.
- Towing companies and locksmiths in the area and many more helpful tips.

Cellular Phones tricks:

I heard that the Miami FBI once opened a cellular phone and computer shop with no questions asked, i.e., social security numbers, credit history, as the last thing drug dealers want to give is his information. The FBI controlled this shop, and they were able to monitor the calls to and from drug dealers and crooks. They knew what frequencies the cell phones transmitted and could easily track where the phone was being used and when to bust in on a deal.

Gang members:

Many gang members join the regular army; they learn how to shoot and how to use guns. They get free assault weapons, free training, free tactics, and free advice on killing, using against rivals and other gang members when they leave the army.

***

My Extensive Training—I Had To Complete:
(The following are all taking from my pass certificates).

1989 Pistol Course: (New York)
 Tactical Pistol Course: Includes weapon placement, ready positions, holster draw, reloads, multiple shots while moving, tactical use of cover, moving targets, shooting with both hands, low light, and night vision shooting.

1998 High-Risk Security Course:
 Advanced Weapon Skills: Including tactical handgun course, HALO[29] arrivals/departures, basic land warfare, open-air rescues, IED[30].
 VIBE. Voice Identity Biometric Exploitation, radio procedure, tactical driving, unarmed combat, and high-risk urban movement.

1999 Basic SWAT Course I and II:
 Safety, firearm review, qualification, team management, stealth probe to contact, multiple entry points, categorizing warrants, breaching techniques, using a protection shield, sniper-initiated assaults, vehicle takedown, and how to deal with barricaded shooters, etc.

1999 S.E.R.E Course:
 This stands for **S**urvival skills, **E**vasion tactics, **R**esistance

---

[29] See glossary
[30] See glossary

qualifications, Escape skills, including how to break free from nylon zip-ties used as handcuffs and break free from duct tape tightly wrapped around your wrists and legs if the enemy captured you.

2000 Mobile Force Protection Course:

Advanced pistol and carbine marksmanship, shooting positions, vehicle cover, terminal ballistics, fire and movement, man down/casualty training, counter-ambush and urban environment training, convoy/group movement, route planning, evasive driving skills, barricade confrontations, night vision goggle driving.

2000 Advanced Sniper Course:

Marksmanship principles, spotting, judging distance, wind collection, (MOA) 'Minute of Angle' accuracy, sniper range card, rural operations, urban operations, camouflage and concealment, low-light applications, unknown long-distance shooting, synchronized shooting, radio techniques, team planning, and mission execution.

Additional courses.

1990 Survival Course:

We were taken by helicopter and given three weeks to survive on basics and reach base, eat from the land, worms, insects, wild boar, etc. We also had our own 100-acre site near Mount Rainier in Washington, where we practised shooting/training on most weekends. The rest of our team went to church to pray for forgiveness for their sins if we shot someone dead.

1986 Pinkerton Private Investigations course:

I passed with Burns and Pinkerton Security, working with Taylor Investigations. I also did and passed a Polygraph course.

Since 1998, I have been a member of the NRA, America's National Rifle Association, and the North America Hunting Club since 1990.

1986 UK Survival Course:

Survival Course on Dartmoor (Where SAS train now)—two weeks marching, camping, and living off the land. Too many shooting courses to list. But the majority of the gun courses were completed at 'The National Rifle Association'

or 'The National Shooting Centre Bisley Camp,' i.e., police shoots, long-range shooting, rifle, pistol shooting, etc.

***

Gun certificates held in the UK:

I held both firearms and shotgun certificates in the UK.

Which were valid for three years.

Firearm Licence.

Max ammunition to be possessed at the one time:

9mm – 500 rounds

.45 – 150 rounds

7.62 – 500 rounds

Max ammunition to be purchased at one time:

9mm – 300 rounds

.45 – 300 rounds

7.62 – 50 rounds

Shotokan Karate:

In January 2016, I passed seventh Dan, black belt, Shichi-Dan, with a formal title of 'Kyoshi Samurai.' Kyoshi, meaning knowledgeable person—persons over sixty can receive this title.

Glossary of Terms

ABSCOND: To run away, escape to avoid arrest, or to leave the jurisdiction of the court.

AK-47: *Kalashnikov.* A gas-operated automatic 7.62x39mm assault rifle was developed in the Soviet Union by Mikhail Kalashnikov.

AMMO: Ammunition.

ANNEXES: Assume ownership, confiscate, convert, impound, seize, take over, or take possession.

AR15: An AR-15 style rifle is a lightweight semi-automatic rifle based on the ArmaLite AR-15 design.

AR16: The AR-16 is a prototype select-fire, gas-operated battle rifle, made by ArmaLite after the US Military adopted and bought the designs of the AR-15 and M16.

ARREST: The taking or being taken into custody by the authority of the law.

BAD RAP: Bad reputation.

BAIL: A recognized guarantee for the court appearance of a defendant, by posting a determined amount of monies with the court; the surety or sureties who secure the release of an individual from legal custody, being thereby responsible for the appearance in court of the said defendant when scheduled to do so.

BAILABLE: That person may be released on bail, allowing the payment of bail.

BAIL BOND: A surety bond (money or property) offered or deposited by a defendant or other persons to ensure the defendant's appearance at trial; a written declaration of the bail undertaking releasing the defendant from detention.

BAIL BONDSMAN: A person who acts as a surety or gives bail for another, usually referred to as 'bail bondsman' or 'bondsman.'

BAIL ENFORCEMENT AGENT: A person sometimes referred to as bounty hunter who represents the interests of a surety or bondsman; one who acts/stands in his/her place and stead to seek, apprehend and return to lawful custody the person(s) who has been charged with a criminal offense and fled the court's jurisdiction on a bail bond obligation; a privately contracted fugitive recovery agent.

BAIL EXONERATION: A term used by a court to describe a bond that is clear of any liability, which means the guarantor can be released of liability on the bail bond. Either by the principal's surrender to the proper authorities or before the day stipulated in the bond. It is sometimes necessary to file a motion designed to exonerate a forfeited bond on a technicality and not based on the defendant's surrender.

B.D.U: Battle Dress Uniform.

BOHICA: (Military slang) Bend Over Here It Comes Again.

BEEPER: A device that emits a short, high-pitched sound on the receiver's device, receiving a signal from a tracker placed under the body of a motor car.

BOMBER JACKET: This is also known as an MA-1 or MA-2 jacket; the jacket was worn by North American pilots, where it is commonly known as a bomber jacket, especially in areas with cold weather. These jackets became popular in the late 1960s with punks, mods, and skinheads. It was a flight jacket created initially for pilots and eventually became part of popular culture and apparel.

BONDED: Bail or bond (in this case, bail and bond mean the same thing) is an amount of money in cash, property, or surety bond to make sure that a person attends all required court appearances. Bonded out allows an arrested person (defendant) to be released from jail until their case is completed.

BOUNTY: Is a sum of money paid as a reward: Is a gratuity reward, or an unusual or additional benefit conferred upon, or compensation paid to, a class of persons.

BREACHED: To make an opening through a door in a wall or fence or attack someone or something behind it.

BRYLCREEM: This is a British brand of hair styling products for men. The first Brylcreem product was a hair cream created in 1928. The cream is an emulsion of water and mineral oil stabilized with beeswax and was very popular with teddy boys, rockers, and greasers, the motorcycle gangs of the 1950s and late 1960s. The name 'greaser' also came from their greased-back hairstyle.

BUBBLE CAR: Isetta three-wheeled motor car with two wheels in front and one wheel at the back, driven on a motorcycle licence. There also was a Messerschmitt Trojan and a Heinkel bubble car produced.

BUCKS: An American dollar is called a 'Buck.'

CCTV: Closed-circuit television.

COLLATERAL: Something of value, such as property, i.e., cars, boats, guns, jewellery or bonds, put up by the defendant or someone acting for the defendant on their behalf to secure the bail bond; if the defendant does not appear on the date set by the court, the collateral is forfeited.

CONCEALED CARRY: where a person carries a firearm that cannot be seen by the casual observer.

CO-SIGNER: Is an individual pledging responsibility as surety on a bail bond undertaking. A co-signer is a person who is obligated to pay back the loan just as the borrower is responsible and obligated to pay back the loan. A co-signer could be your spouse, a parent, or a friend—an individual pledging responsibility as surety on a bail bond undertaking.

CV: This is an abbreviation for Curriculum Vitae. Suppose a job advertisement asks for a CV. In that case, that's a hint that the employer expects a great deal of life experience and accomplishments, including education, original research, presentations you've given, and papers or books you've had published.

D.E.A: Drug Enforcement Agency. Formed during the summer of 1973, the DEA is a federal law enforcement agency responsible for dealing with drug smuggling and drug abuse within the United States. The DEA is responsible for inhibiting drug trafficking within the United States of America.

DEFENDANT: Is a person in a court of law who is accused of having done something wrong.

DISCHARGE: This is to release the surety from a bail bond responsibility.

DOJO: A room or hall in which karate, judo, and other martial arts are practiced.

DOMINION: The control over a country or people, or the land that belongs to a ruler.

DRIVE-BY SHOOTING: This is a type of assault that usually involves the perpetrators firing a weapon from within a motor vehicle and then fleeing. Such shootings are associated with gang violence in urban areas of the United States.

DRIZZLING: To rain in small light drops.

E.P.A: The Environmental Protection Agency. The EPA exists to protect human health and the environment.

EXONERATION: (See Discharge).

F.B.I: Federal Bureau of Investigation. Operating under the United States Department of Justice jurisdiction, the FBI is also a member of the U.S. Intelligence Community and reports to both the Attorney General and the Director of National Intelligence.

FEDERAL BAIL: Federal charges originate in federal courts. A federal judge has the ability to set a bail or bond amount, just like a state judge does. Those facing charges in a federal court may be met with a higher bond amount than a state court may have charged for a similar offense

FELON: someone who has committed a crime.

FELONY: In the United States, where the felony/misdemeanor distinction is still widely applied, the federal government defines a felony as a crime punishable by death or imprisonment in excess of one year: a serious crime that can be punished by more than one year in prison.

FLASHLIGHT: Torch or hand-held light.

FORFEITURE NOTICE: Bond forfeiture, law, and legal definition. A forfeited bond becomes the jurisdiction's property overseeing the case, and it cannot be refunded. In criminal cases, bail bond forfeiture arises when a defendant, whose appearance in court has been guaranteed by the posting of a bond, fails to appear in court on that date.

F.T.A: Failure to Appear. A person charged with a crime did not appear in court on a date and time set by the court.

FUGITIVE: A person who flees, runs, or has escaped from justice.

GANG BANGER-MEMBER: Definition of a gangbanger is a slang term for a member of a street gang.

GI: 'Karate-gi' is the formal Japanese name for the traditional uniform used for Karate and other martial arts practice and competition.

HALO: High Altitude-Low Opening. In the HALO technique, the parachutist wears breathing equipment and opens his parachute at a low altitude after free-falling for a long time.

HAZMAT: It is an abbreviation for hazardous materials.

HOBO: A homeless person; a bum, tramp, or vagrant.

HORN DOG: Sexually aggressive man or a man with strong sexual desires.

IED: Improvised Explosive Device.

INTEL: Intelligence.

INTERSTATE: One of a vast system of motorways running between the US states.

JAPS: Japanese.

JURISDICTION: The authority given by law to a court to try cases and rule on legal matters within a particular geographic area and over specific legal claims. It is vital to determine before a lawsuit is filed which court has jurisdiction.

LICENCE PLATE: Car number plate.

LIMEY: A word Americans use to describe an English or British person.

LOTHARIOS: A fast-talking gigolo or womanizer; Is a man who behaves selfishly and irresponsibly in his sexual relationships with women.

M16: The M16 rifle. Caliber 5.56 mm, a United States military adaptation of the ArmaLite AR-15 rifle. The original M16 was a 5.56mm automatic rifle with a 20-round magazine.

MAOA GENE: Monoamine Oxidase-A gene. This gene was named the 'warrior gene' in 2004. It is a survival gene that is passed down by family generations. Studies have linked the 'warrior gene' to an increased risk-taking and retaliatory behaviour. One emerging aspect of recent advances in Neurocriminology is discovering possible links between violent criminal behaviour and genetics. Men with the 'warrior gene' are more likely to respond aggressively to a perceived conflict.

MERCENARY: As a Soldier of fortune, an individual is hired to serve in a foreign army to participate in an armed conflict but is not part of a regular army or other governmental military force.

METH: Methamphetamine. The drug belongs to a family of amphetamines, powerful stimulants that speed up the body's central nervous system.

MISDEMEANOR: A misdemeanor is considered a crime of low seriousness. In the United States, the federal government generally considers a crime punishable with incarceration for one year or less to be a misdemeanor.

MOTION TO VACATE FORFEITURE: A formal written request to the court to set aside the forfeiture notice sent to the surety when the defendant failed to appear based upon the surety's producing the defendant to the court or other extenuating circumstances.

NADA: Nothing, zero.

NICKLE AND DIME JOBS: Involving or paying only a small amount of money.

N.C.I.C.: National Crime Information Center.

N.S.P.C.C: National Society for the Prevention of Cruelty to Children.

OBITER DICTA or DICTUM: It is a judge's expression of opinion uttered in court or written judgments, but not essential to the decision, and therefore not legally binding as a precedent, as it is an incidental remark. The word 'obiter dicta' is a Latin word, which means 'things said by the way.'

ODOROUS: Giving off or having an odour of a foul smell about it.

OPEN CARRY: In the United States, open carry refers to the practice of 'openly carrying a firearm in a public place on full view in a holster, or otherwise.'

PRINCIPAL: Defendant accused of a crime and released on a bail bond.

RAIN CHECK: To make an arrangement to do a said activity at another time.

REAR FENDER: Fender is the American English term for the part of an automobile, motorcycle, or other vehicle body that frames a wheel well (the fender underside). Its primary purpose is to prevent sand, mud, rocks, liquids, and other road spray from being thrown into the air by the rotating tire a mudguard.

RECOGNIZANCE (OWN): The Release of a detained individual into his own custody and surety responsibility; release from custody on basis and scope of residential, employment, and other bail release criteria.

RED NECK: In America, it is a derogatory term name for a poor, white person without education, especially a hillbilly or one living in the countryside in the southern US, who is believed to have prejudiced unreasonable ideas and beliefs. They disapprove of them because they think he is uneducated and has strong, unjustified opinions; one is regarded as ignorant, bigoted, violent, etc.

RESUME: (See CV) The purpose of a resume summarises your skills, abilities, and accomplishments. It is a quick advertisement for who you are. It is a 'snapshot' of you to capture and emphasize interests and secure you an interview.

SABBATH: A Holy day, the Sabbath is a day of delightful communion with God and one another.

SENSEI: Is a martial arts teacher.

SHTUM: To be or become quiet and non-communicative. Stay silent, quiet, not speaking.

SIDEWALK: Pavement or pedestrian path beside a road.

SKIP(S): Fugitives that fail to appear on their court date and that can't be found at their place of residence or usual hangouts.

SKIP TRACER: Skip tracing is an industry term used to describe the process of locating a fugitive that can't be found at their place of residence or usual hangouts. The act of skip tracing is most often used by bail bondsmen, bounty hunters, repossession agents, private investigators, debt collectors, and even journalists.

SNAFU: (Military slang) Situation Normal All Fucked Up.

SNOWFLAKE: The word was added to the Oxford English Dictionary in 2018. The name became popular in 2016 when some older generations scoffed at young people's "hysterical" reaction to the EU referendum result. The term *snowflake* is now used as an insult to describe overly sensitive someone or has a feeling entitled to special treatment or consideration'. In other words, self-obsessed and fragile, easily offended, has an inflated sense of uniqueness or an unwarranted sense of entitlement. They are overly-emotional, easily offended, or unable to deal with opposing opinions. Today's generation of sensitive university students are often labelled snowflakes; they gasp in horror when they hear an idea they don't like and believe they have a right to be protected from anything unpalatable.

SOUTHERN DRAWL: Southern drawl vowel breaking. All three stages of the Southern Shift often result in the short front pure vowels being 'broken' into gliding vowels, making one-syllable words like 'pet' and 'pit' sound as if they might have two syllables as something like pay-it and pee-it, respectively.

SURETY(S): Individual(s) who undertakes to pay money or do any other act in the event said the principal fails to appear. A contract between the principal and the guarantor agrees to pay the court the sum of money affixed by the set court bail.

SURVEILLANCE: The act of watching a person or a place, significantly if that person is believed to be involved with criminal activity or a place where criminals gather: 'The parking lot is kept under video surveillance.' Often, a person suspected of something illegal by the authorities is placed under surveillance, meaning they are closely watched to see if their suspicions are well-founded.

S.W.A.T (Special Weapons and Tactics): A law enforcement unit that uses specialized or military equipment and tactics. First created in the 1960s to handle riot control or violent confrontations with criminals.

TARFU: (Military slang) Totally And Royally Fucked Up.

TASER: A 'Taser' is the brand name of an electroshock weapon. (The company used to be called 'Taser International.' It is now called Axon Enterprise Inc.) The Taser fires two small dart-like electrodes, which stay connected to the central unit by conductors or wires, to deliver an electric current to disrupt voluntary control of a person's muscles, causing 'neuromuscular incapacitation.'

TAWDY: Showy, but cheap and of low quality, Sordid or unpleasant.

THERMOS: Vacuum flask. It is an insulating storage vessel that considerably lengthens the time over which its contents remain hotter or cooler than the flask's surroundings.

WINDSHIELD: Windscreen. A front transparent screen of glass that protects the occupants of a vehicle.

YANKS: A term used by the British to describe all Americans.

Now all the Action Starts:

**Cases to Read in Book 2
'Dead or Alive'
How a British Bounty Hunter
took America by Storm.**

Two Rides
Not Today, Dewayne
Me? Ride Shotgun?
A Midnight Run
Down Below the Border
A Man's Best Friend
Living out a Boyhood Dream
The Stripper
Did He Have a Gun—or Didn't He?
Mother's Boy
Sha' Dawg
You May Run, but You Can't Fly
Wipe Your Own Damned Ass!
Sure, I'll Do You a Favour
Freight Train, Freight Train, Goin' So Fast
A City in Flames
Size Isn't Everything
Meet Dan Durass
It's Your Thanksgiving, Not Mine
A Few Facts about Bounty Hunters
Interesting Facts